D1068874

GUARDIANSHIP, CONSERVATORSHIP AND THE LAW

by

Margaret C. Jasper

Oceana's Legal Almanac Series:
Law for the Layperson

Oceana®

NEW YORK

OXFORD

UNIVERSITY PRESS

*Oxford University Press, Inc., publishes works that further Oxford University's
objective of excellence in research, scholarship, and education.*

Copyright © 2008 by Oxford University Press, Inc.
Published by Oxford University Press, Inc.
198 Madison Avenue, New York, New York 10016

Oxford is a registered trademark of Oxford University Press
Oceana is a registered trademark of Oxford University Press, Inc.

Library of Congress Cataloging-in-Publication Data

Jasper, Margaret C.
  Guardianship, conservatorship, and the law / by Margaret C. Jasper.
    p. cm. -- (Oceana's legal almanac series: law for the layperson)
  ISBN 978-0-19-533899-7 (alk. paper)
    1. Guardian and ward--United States. 2. Conservatorships--United States.
I. Title.
  KF553.Z9J37 2008
  346.7301'8--dc22

                                                                2008000334

Note to Readers:

This publication is designed to provide accurate and authoritative information in regard to
the subject matter covered. It is based upon sources believed to be accurate and reliable and
is intended to be current as of the time it was written. It is sold with the understanding that
the publisher is not engaged in rendering legal, accounting, or other professional services. If
legal advice or other expert assistance is required, the services of a competent professional
person should be sought. Also, to confirm that the information has not been affected or
changed by recent developments, traditional legal research techniques should be used, including checking primary sources where appropriate.

*(Based on the Declaration of Principles jointly adopted by a Committee of the
American Bar Association and a Committee of Publishers and Associations.)*

> You may order this or any other Oxford University Press publication
> by visiting the Oxford University Press website at www.oup.com

To My Husband Chris

Your love and support

are my motivation and inspiration

To My Sons, Michael, Nick and Chris

-and-

In memory of my son, Jimmy

Table of Contents

CHAPTER 3:
GUARDIANSHIP OF AN INCAPACITATED ADULT

ABOUT THE AUTHOR

MARGARET C. JASPER is an attorney engaged in the general practice of law in South Salem, New York, concentrating in the areas of personal injury and entertainment law. Ms. Jasper holds a Juris Doctor degree from Pace University School of Law, White Plains, New York, is a member of the New York and Connecticut bars, and is certified to practice before the United States District Courts for the Southern and Eastern Districts of New York, the United States Court of Appeals for the Second Circuit, and the United States Supreme Court.

Ms. Jasper has been appointed to the law guardian panel for the Family Court of the State of New York, is a member of a number of professional organizations and associations, and is a New York State licensed real estate broker operating as Jasper Real Estate, in South Salem, New York.

Margaret Jasper maintains a website at http://www.JasperLawOffice. com.

In 2004, Ms. Jasper successfully argued a case before the New York Court of Appeals, which gives mothers of babies who are stillborn due to medical negligence, the right to bring a legal action and recover emotional distress damages. This successful appeal overturned a 26-year old New York case precedent, which previously prevented mothers of stillborn babies from suing their negligent medical providers.

Ms. Jasper is the author and general editor of the following legal almanacs:

Adoption Law

AIDS Law

The Americans with Disabilities Act

Animal Rights Law

Auto Leasing

Bankruptcy Law for the Individual Debtor

Banks and their Customers

Becoming a Citizen

Buying and Selling Your Home

Commercial Law

Consumer Rights and the Law

Co-ops and Condominiums: Your Rights and Obligations As Owner

Copyright Law

Credit Cards and the Law

Custodial Rights

Dealing with Debt

Dictionary of Selected Legal Terms

Drunk Driving Law

DWI, DUI and the Law

Education Law

Elder Law

Employee Rights in the Workplace

Employment Discrimination Under Title VII

Environmental Law

Estate Planning

Everyday Legal Forms

Executors and Personal Representatives: Rights and Responsibilities

Harassment in the Workplace

Health Care and Your Rights

Health Care Directives

Hiring Household Help and Contractors: Your Rights and Obligations Under the Law

Home Mortgage Law Primer

Hospital Liability Law

How To Change Your Name

How To Form an LLC

How To Protect Your Challenged Child

How To Start Your Own Business

Identity Theft and How To Protect Yourself

Individual Bankruptcy and Restructuring

Injured on the Job: Employee Rights, Worker's Compensation and Disability Insurance Law

International Adoption

Juvenile Justice and Children's Law

Labor Law

Landlord-Tenant Law

Law for the Small Business Owner

The Law of Attachment and Garnishment

The Law of Buying and Selling

The Law of Capital Punishment

The Law of Child Custody

The Law of Contracts

The Law of Debt Collection

The Law of Dispute Resolution

The Law of Guardianship and Conservatorship

The Law of Immigration

The Law of Libel and Slander

The Law of Medical Malpractice

The Law of No-Fault Insurance

The Law of Obscenity and Pornography

The Law of Personal Injury

The Law of Premises Liability

The Law of Product Liability

The Law of Speech and the First Amendment

Lemon Laws

Living Together: Practical Legal Issues

Marriage and Divorce

Missing and Exploited Children: How to Protect Your Child

Motor Vehicle Law

Nursing Home Negligence

Patent Law

Pet Law

Prescription Drugs

Privacy and the Internet: Your Rights and Expectations Under the Law

Probate Law

Protecting Your Business: Disaster Preparation and the Law

Real Estate Law for the Homeowner and Broker

Religion and the Law

Retirement Planning

The Right to Die

Rights of Single Parents

Small Claims Court

Social Security Law

Special Education Law

Teenagers and Substance Abuse

Trademark Law

Trouble Next Door: What to do With Your Neighbor

Victim's Rights Law

Violence Against Women

Welfare: Your Rights and the Law

What if It Happened to You: Violent Crimes and Victims' Rights

What if the Product Doesn't Work: Warranties & Guarantees

Workers' Compensation Law

Your Child's Legal Rights: An Overview

Your Rights in a Class Action Suit

Your Rights as a Tenant

Your Rights Under the Family and Medical Leave Act

You've Been Fired: Your Rights and Remedies

INTRODUCTION

Until a child reaches the legal age of majority, he or she is considered legally incapable of taking care of his or her personal needs, or of managing his or her finances. If a child does not have a parent who is willing or able to care for him or her, the state may appoint a "guardian" to fill the parental role and protect the child. The minor is referred to as the "ward" of the guardian.

Once a person reaches the legal age of majority, he or she is presumed by law to be legally competent, and able to manage his or her affairs. However, when an adult, due to physical or mental incapacity or incompetence, is no longer able to manage his or her affairs, or function safely in society, the state may appoint a "conservator" who will manage that person's affairs on his or her behalf. The legally incapacitated person is known as a "conservatee."

This Almanac discusses the appointment of a guardian and a conservator, and their respective duties. The manner in which a court determines incapacity is examined. Termination of a guardianship or conservatorship is also discussed. In addition, this Almanac explores alternatives to guardianship, including advance directives, trust funds, social security representative payees, and adult protective services.

The Appendix provides statutory citations, applicable forms, and other pertinent information and data. The Glossary contains definitions of many of the terms used throughout the Almanac

CHAPTER 1:
AN OVERVIEW OF GUARDIANSHIPS AND CONSERVATORSHIPS

THE INDIVIDUAL'S RIGHT TO SELF-DETERMINATION

The right to make decisions regarding one's personal affairs, and to manage one's property, is a fundamental right of every American citizen. However, hundreds of thousands of adults are denied these basic rights, and lose all control of their personal and financial affairs.

Once a court determines that an individual is legally incompetent or incapacitated, a guardian or conservator is appointed to make decisions on behalf of that individual. Unfortunately, research has revealed that many of those individuals who have been deprived of their right to independent decision-making, are not being adequately treated.

It is an unfortunate reality that many persons and agencies appointed to manage the personal and financial affairs for mentally incapacitated individuals do not make decisions that are in the best interests of the ward or conservatee and, in some cases, actually exploit these individuals.

An improperly conducted guardianship or conservatorship can result in fraud and thievery, and can jeopardize the health and safety of the ward or conservatee, particularly when non-family members are appointed as guardians or conservators.

On the other hand, depending on the degree of disability, a properly conducted guardianship or conservatorship may allow the individual to participate in the management of his or her finances and health care, and allow the individual a certain degree of autonomy.

For this reason, it is essential that the appointment of a guardian or conservator be made with the utmost care, and that there is careful and ongoing oversight of this relationship. The proposed guardian or conservator must be required to comply with the duties and responsibilities as directed by the appointing court. A guardian or conservator, as a fiduciary, is required to act at all times in the best interests of the ward or conservatee.

ADVANCE PLANNING FOR INCAPACITY

Although a properly administered guardianship or conservatorship can be beneficial and work in the best interests of an incapacitated individual, it is better to avoid this option if at all possible.

Incapacity generally refers to an individual's inability to make reasonable and sound decisions regarding his or her personal and financial affairs. This scenario is not limited to senior citizens. A disabling condition—e.g., a serious illness or accident—can happen to any person at any time. When such a tragedy occurs, it can create serious problems for loved ones, who must now stand in the shoes of the incapacitated individual, and make decisions that are in their loved one's best interests.

For example, if an individual becomes incapacitated, and has never appointed another person to make legal or medical decisions on his or her behalf, it may result in disputes among family members regarding how to handle the incapacitated individual's personal, medical and financial affairs. Often, a guardian or conservator must be appointed to make these important decisions.

There are a number of alternatives you can choose that will avoid the necessity of such legal proceedings. Once you have determined how you would want certain situations handled—e.g., management of your health care and finances—and the individual you trust to make those decisions on your behalf, you should consult an attorney to discuss the various options available.

Alternatives to guardianship and conservatorship are discussed more fully in Chapter 6, "Conservatorship; Protecting the Property of the Ward," of this Almanac.

GUARDIANSHIP AND CONSERVATORSHIP DEFINED

A guardian is a court-appointed official who may be appointed to care for unemancipated minors who have lost their parents to death or incapacitation or for whom parental authority has been legally terminated. Guardians may also be appointed to care for adults who have become incapacitated and who cannot, therefore, take care of themselves.

A conservator is a court-appointed official who may be appointed to receive, invest, manage, and disburse property held for a minor or an incapacitated person. Conservators are fiduciaries who must receive, invest, manage and disburse property in the best interests of the protected person.

Conservators will not be appointed in every case in which a minor or incapacitated person has property that must be managed. A conservator is likely to be appointed only when there is a sufficient quantity and quality of property to warrant the creation of a court-supervised conservatorship.

TERMINOLOGY

Depending on the jurisdiction, the term guardianship is generally defined as a legal relationship between a capable adult, known as a "guardian," and a "ward"—i.e., an individual who, by reason of infancy or legal disability, is unable to care for his or her own personal needs and/or manage his or her financial resources.

In this area of law, state statutes vary in their terminology, which may be somewhat confusing. In most states, the person who manages the personal needs of the ward is known as a "guardian" whereas the person responsible for managing the ward's financial resources is known as a "conservator."

In other states, the term "guardian" refers to the individual responsible for managing the needs and finances of a minor ward, and the term "conservator" refers to the individual responsible for managing the needs and finances of an adult ward.

In addition, depending on the state, the individual who is the subject of the proposed guardianship or conservatorship is referred to by different names, e.g., "an allegedly incapacitated person," "a proposed ward," or "a proposed conservatee."

Following establishment of the guardianship or conservatorship, this individual may be called a "ward," "conservatee," "protected person," or "interdict," depending on the jurisdiction.

To add to the confusion, state laws differ as to the criteria and procedure for appointing a guardian or conservator, and the manner in which the guardianship or conservatorship is monitored. Although there are national guidelines, it is not mandatory that the states follow them. The states are free to adopt the guidelines, in whole or in part, or to simply reject them altogether.

Regardless of the terminology used and the procedures followed, guardianships and conservatorships are established to protect vulnerable persons from abuse, neglect and exploitation, to provide for their personal care, and to manage their finances and property.

For purposes of this Almanac, the term "guardian" will be used to refer to the individual appointed to care for an unemancipated minor or an incapacitated adult, known as a "ward," and the term "conservator" will be used to refer to the person who is appointed to manage the property of the ward.

THE UNIFORM PROBATE CODE

In 1968, the Uniform Probate Code (UPC) was drafted by the National Conference of Commissioners on Uniform State Laws (NCCUSL). The UPC governs all aspects of the probate process. In 1982, Article 5 of the UPC was extensively revised. Article 5 provides for the appointment and supervision of guardians and conservators for minors and incapacitated adults.

Under the UPC, no adult can be subjected to a guardianship or conservatorship without a determination of incapacity by a court. In addition, the UPC provides that all guardians and conservators are subject to the jurisdiction and the supervision of the court.

THE UNIFORM GUARDIANSHIP AND PROTECTIVE PROCEEDINGS ACT

The Uniform Guardianship and Protective Proceedings Act (UGPPA) was drafted by the NCCUSL in 1982 as a free-standing act. The UGPPA is derived from Article 5 of the Uniform Probate Code.

In 1997, the UGPPA was extensively revised. The UGPPPA sets forth procedures for the appointment of guardians and conservators for minors and incapacitated person, and describes the powers, duties and liabilities of guardians and conservators.

The UGPPA also emphasizes due process and fair proceedings for incapacitated persons, and supports limiting the power of guardians and conservators. The goal is to find a balance between the power of the guardian or conservator, while still protecting the person subjected to that power.

As of 2007, the UGPPA has been adopted by Alabama, Colorado, Hawaii, Minnesota, and Montana. In addition, the American Bar Association approved UPPGA as an appropriate Act for those states desiring to adopt the specific substantive law suggested in the Act.

THE UNIFORM ADULT GUARDIANSHIP AND PROTECTIVE PROCEEDINGS JURISDICTION ACT

There are more than fifty guardianship systems in the United States, which creates frequent problems when determining jurisdiction. In 2007, in response to this problem, the NCCUSL drafted the Uniform Adult Guardianship and Protective Proceedings Jurisdiction Act (UAGPPJA). The UAGPPJA addresses the issue of jurisdiction over adult guardianships, conservatorships and other protective proceedings, and provides a mechanism for resolving these multi-state jurisdictional disputes.

The UAGPPJA contains specific guidelines to specify which court has jurisdiction to appoint a guardian or conservator for an incapacitated adult. The goal of the Act is that only one state will have jurisdiction over the proceedings at any one time.

CHAPTER 2:
GUARDIANSHIP OF A MINOR

IN GENERAL

The legal parent of a minor child is also referred to as the child's "natural guardian." A guardianship occurs when a court appoints an adult (the "guardian") to take care of an unemancipated minor (the "ward") whose parents are unable or unwilling to care for the child. Once appointed, the legal guardian has the same legal responsibilities as a parent.

Many adults who have physical custody of a child do not file for legal guardianship status for a number of reasons. For example, the child's parents may not want to consent to a legal guardianship, particularly if it is a temporary arrangement.

An individual can still act as a child's caregiver without being appointed the child's legal guardian by a court if the parents sign a notarized affidavit giving the caregiver permission to make decisions about the child's education and medical care.

A sample guardianship authorization affidavit is set forth at Appendix 1.

Nevertheless, filing a petition for legal guardianship may be preferable. For example, the guardianship authorization affidavit may not be accepted in all situations, e.g., schools, insurance carriers, and medical facilities may require proof of legal guardianship. In addition, the parents can cancel the affidavit at anytime.

Before filing a petition for legal guardianship, you should consider whether you are prepared for such an undertaking, as you will be legally responsible for the child. You must also consider the impact a guardianship will have on your existing family.

In order to qualify as a legal guardian, the proposed guardian must generally be at least 18 years of age and a citizen or legal resident of the United States. In addition, the proposed guardian should be in good health and must have no history of child abuse or neglect.

PURPOSE

Guardianship for a minor is generally sought because a child is living with an adult who is not the child's parent, and the adult needs the legal authority to make decisions on behalf of the child. The court-appointed guardian has full legal and physical custody of the child. A legal guardian may need to be appointed if:

1. The child's parent died;

2. The child's parent became disabled and unable to care for the child;

3. The parent abandoned the child; or

4. The child's parent will be absent for a prolonged period of time, e.g., military duty, deportation, or imprisonment.

The court may require the guardian to assist the child in maintaining a relationship with his or her parents. This may include the parent's right to visitation with the child, although the court may place certain restrictions on these rights, depending on the circumstances, e.g., the court may order supervised visitation.

DUTIES AND RESPONSIBILITIES

The legal guardian of the person of a child has full legal and physical custody of the child, and is responsible for making all decisions relating to the child. In general, the guardian also has the same responsibilities as the birth parent, as set forth below.

Basic Responsibilities

The guardian is in charge of the care, custody, and control of the child. The guardian is responsible for providing for food, clothing, shelter, education, and all the medical and dental needs of the child. In addition, the legal guardian must provide for the safety, protection, and physical and emotional growth of the child.

Custody

The guardian has full legal and physical custody of the child and is responsible for all decisions relating to the child. The child's parents can no longer make decisions for the child while there is a guardianship. The parents' rights are suspended—not terminated—as long as a guardian is appointed for a minor. The guardian may, but is not required to, solicit input from the parents concerning major decisions.

Education

The guardian is responsible for the child's education. The guardian must determine where the child should attend school. As the child's advocate within the school system, the legal guardian should attend conferences and play an active role in the child's education.

For younger children, the guardian may consider enrolling the child in an early childhood program. For older children, the guardian should consider the child's future educational needs, such as college or trade school. The guardian must assist the child in obtaining services if the child has special educational needs, and should help the child in setting and attaining his or her educational goals.

Residence

The guardian has the right to determine where the child lives. The child will normally live with the guardian; however, when necessary, the guardian is allowed to make other arrangements if it is in the best interest of the child.

The guardian should obtain court approval before placing the child back with his or her parents. The guardian does not have the right to change the child's residence to a place outside of the state without court permission. If the court grants permission, state law generally requires that the guardian establish legal guardianship in the state where the child will be living. Individual states have different rules regarding guardianships, therefore, the reader is advised to seek additional information about relocation in the state where he or she wants the child to live.

Medical Treatment

The legal guardian has the authority to consent to the child's medical treatment. However, if the child is 14 years or older, except in emergencies, surgery may not be performed on the child unless either:

(1) both the child and the guardian consent; or

(2) a court order is obtained that specifically authorizes the surgery.

In addition, a guardian may not place a child involuntarily in a mental health treatment facility under a mental health guardianship. A mental health guardianship proceeding is required for an involuntary commitment. However, the guardian may secure counseling and other necessary mental health services for the child. The law also allows older and more mature children to consent to their own treatment in certain situations, e.g., outpatient mental health treatment; medical care related to pregnancy or sexually transmitted diseases; and drug and alcohol treatment.

Support and Services

Regardless of the guardianship, the child's parents are still obligated to financially support the child. If the parents fail to pay child support, the guardian can petition the court for child support.

The child may also be eligible for Temporary Aid for Needy Families (TANF), formerly known as AFDC; social security benefits; Veterans Administration benefits; Indian child welfare benefits; and other public or private funds.

There are agencies in each county that may be helpful in meeting the specific needs of children who come from conflicted, troubled, or deprived environments. If the child has special needs, you must strive to meet those needs or secure appropriate services.

Visitation

The court may require that the guardian allow visitation or contact between the child and his or her parents. The child's needs often require that the parent-child relationship be maintained, within reason. However, the court may place restrictions on the visits, such as the requirement of supervision. The court may also impose other conditions in the child's best interest.

Driver's License

The guardian has the authority to consent to the minor's application for a driver's license. If the guardian consents, he or she will become liable for any civil damages that may result if the minor causes an accident.

Military Service

The guardian may consent to the minor's enlistment in the armed services. If the minor enters into active duty with the armed forces, the minor generally becomes emancipated under state law.

Marriage

For the minor to marry, the guardian—and usually the court—must give permission. If the minor enters a valid marriage, the minor generally becomes emancipated under state law.

Misconduct

A guardian, like a parent, is liable for the harm and damages caused by the willful misconduct of a child.

Additional Responsibilities

The court may place other conditions on the guardianship or additional duties upon the guardian. For example, the court may require the guardian to complete counseling or parenting classes, to obtain specific services for the child, or to follow a scheduled visitation plan between the child and the child's parents or relatives. The legal guardian must follow all court orders.

THE GUARDIANSHIP PETITION

Filing the Petition

In order to become a child's legal guardian, a petition must be filed with the appropriate court. In an emergency, a petition for temporary guardianship may be filed in the interim.

Generally, the petition must include the following information:

1. The name and address of the proposed guardian;

2. The name, address and date of birth of the child;

3. The name and address of the child's natural parents or the individuals who have been caring for the child; and

4. The reasons guardianship is being sought for the child.

A sample petition for guardianship of a minor is set forth at Appendix 2.

There is usually a fee for filing the guardianship petition. In addition, there may be a fee for the required investigation. The petitioner may request a waiver of fees from the court if he or she is unable to afford the fees.

Determining the Venue

Venue for the guardianship proceeding is generally in the county of the state where the child resides or is present at the time the petition is filed.

Notice Requirement

The prospective guardian must provide notice of his or her petition for guardianship and notice of the date and time of the guardianship hearing by serving a copy of these papers upon certain individuals, which may include:

1. The child's mother, if she is living;

2. The child's father, if he is living and paternity has been established;

3. The person with whom the child lives; and

4. The child, if over a certain age, e.g., 14. However, if the child is physically, mentally or developmentally disabled and is unable to

give informed consent, the court may appoint a lawyer—also referred to as a "guardian ad litem—to act on behalf of the child.

If the child is in foster care, notice should be served upon the social services agency having jurisdiction over the child, and the child's foster parents, if any.

Notice must be provided within a certain number of days prior to the date of the hearing set by the court.

Generally, a professional process server should be hired to serve the papers, although most courts permit any person over the age of 18 to serve the papers. After the papers are served, the person who served the papers must complete an affidavit of service, which must be submitted to the court as proof of compliance with the notice requirement.

A sample notice of the guardianship hearing is set forth at Appendix 3.

Consent Requirement

The following individuals must generally consent to the appointment of a legal guardian:

1. Both parents, if they were married at the time the child was born;

2. The mother only, if she is unmarried and the father has not been identified;

3. The father, even if he was not married to the mother at the time the child was born, provided:

(a) Paternity has been established;

(b) The father was named on the child's birth certificate;

(c) The father has registered with the state's putative father registry;

(d) The father has been involved with the child during the child's life. Under certain circumstances, the court may appoint a legal guardian for the child even if the parents object to the appointment.

THE GUARDIANSHIP INVESTIGATION

As part of the guardianship proceeding, the court will appoint a neutral investigator to investigate the situation and all of the parties involved. Upon completion of the investigation, the investigator will provide the court with a written report. The report will include the investigator's recommendations and any concerns the investigator may have concerning the proposed guardianship.

The Home Study

As part of the investigation, a home study will likely be conducted. In general, a home study may include:

1. A visit to the prospective guardian's home where the child will be living;

2. A personal interview with the prospective guardian;

3. A personal interview with the child;

4. A thorough review of all documents relating to the child, including medical and school records, etc.;

5. Contact with references;

6. A criminal record check of the prospective guardian and all adults living in the home; and

7. A check of the state child abuse and neglect registry of the prospective guardian and all adults living in the home.

THE GUARDIANSHIP HEARING

A guardianship hearing will be held at which time the court will review the case and decide whether to grant the prospective guardian's petition. The court will make its determination based on the best interests of the child.

If the parents do not want the petitioner appointed as legal guardian, the court may not approve the petition. However, if the parents have abandoned the child, or if the court determines that it would be detrimental to the child if he or she is left in the parents' care, the court may approve the petition regardless of the parents' opposition.

The court may also attempt to have the child's parents and the prospective guardian reach an agreement, particularly if there are no issues of abuse or neglect.

LETTERS OF GUARDIANSHIP

Upon conclusion of the hearing, the judge will consider all of the evidence supporting the petition for guardianship, as well as any opposition to the petition. If the petition is approved, the court will issue letters of guardianship and an order appointing the guardian. Letters of guardianship prove that the individual has been appointed legal guardian over the minor child.

Sample letters of guardianship and an order appointing a guardian of a minor are set forth at Appendix 4 and 5, respectively.

The guardian may be required to file an acceptance of the appointment with the court along with any required bond.

Either a certified or authenticated copy of the letters of guardianship may serve as proof of authority by appointment. This document may be necessary to assist the guardian in carrying out his or her responsibilities, e.g., when seeking medical care for the child.

Limitations

Any limits on the powers of the guardian must be stated in the letters of guardianship. Third parties are charged with knowledge of the restrictions endorsed on the letters of guardianship, and are subject to possible liability for failing to act in accordance with those restrictions.

TERMINATION OF THE LEGAL GUARDIANSHIP

Duration

The guardianship generally lasts until:

1. The child reaches 18 years of age;

2. The child is adopted;

2. The child marries;

3. The child is declared emancipated by the court;

4. The child enters military service; or

5. The child dies.

If the child is physically, mentally or developmentally disabled, the guardianship may continue as long as the child needs someone to take care of his or her needs.

Removal

The legal guardian may be removed for a number of reasons, or when it is in the child's best interests. Removal may occur as a result of a petition filed by the child, the child's parents, another interested person, or on the court's own motion.

In order to terminate the guardianship, it must be shown that the guardianship is no longer necessary, or is not in the best interests of the child.

Resignation

An individual may resign as guardian of the child. Generally, there must be a hearing, and notice of the hearing must be served upon all interested persons. In order to resign, you must demonstrate to the court that it will be in the child's best interests if you resign. If your request is approved, another guardian will be appointed for the minor.

ADOPTION DISTINGUISHED

A legal guardianship is not the same as adoption, and the legal guardian does not have the same rights as an adoptive parent. For example, a legal guardian does not become the child's parent, and the legal relationship between the birth parent and the child continues. In an adoption, the legal relationship between the birth parent and child ends, and the adoptive parent becomes the child's legal parent.

In addition, in a legal guardianship, the child's birth name remains the same, whereas in an adoption, the name on the child's birth certificate is generally changed to that of the adoptive parents. Further, in a legal guardianship, the child is entitled to receive benefits through his or her birth parents, such as social security payments or child support. An adoptive child has no rights to such benefits nor do the birth parents have any right to the child's property once the adoption is finalized.

CHAPTER 3:
GUARDIANSHIP OF AN
INCAPACITATED ADULT

IN GENERAL

A guardian is an individual appointed by the court to care for an incapacitated person. An incapacitated person is an adult who has been found by a court to lack the physical and/or mental capacity to care for him or herself, and who is found to be incapable of caring for his or her property. The guardian makes decisions regarding the personal affairs of the incapacitated person, who is known as a ward. In making those decisions, the guardian is required to ensure that the best interests of the ward are represented.

DETERMINING INCAPACITY

The definition of an incapacitated person is based on the individual's functional abilities. Some individuals may be able to handle certain tasks, while needing assistance with performing others. Before a guardian may be appointed, the individual must be determined to be incapacitated.

Pursuant to Section 102(5) of the Uniform Guardianship and Protective Persons Act, this means that the individual is "unable to receive and evaluate information or make or communicate decisions to such an extent that the individual lacks the ability to meet essential requirements for physical health, safety, or self-care, even with appropriate technological assistance." If there is available technology that will allow the individual to "receive and evaluate information" or "make or communicate decisions," then the individual may not be deemed incapacitated.

When petitioning for guardianship, the prospective guardian will be required to describe the proposed ward's mental or physical health, and state why he or she believes there is a need for a conservatorship.

DUTIES AND RESPONSIBILITIES

Once appointed, the guardian derives certain powers and duties from applicable state statutes. In some instances, the guardian exercises complete decision-making over both the personal and financial affairs of the ward—known as plenary power. This generally includes the right to exercise complete authority over the care, custody and control of the ward.

This power places quite a restraint on the ward, as it may take away previously enjoyed rights, such as the right to vote. Further, it gives the guardian the power to make personal decisions on behalf of the ward, including those concerning living arrangements, medical care, clothing and other needs. Because the appointment of a guardian is a restriction on one's civil liberties, it is a very important determination that should not be ordered unnecessarily.

The guardian is responsible for the personal affairs of the incapacitated person, and must generally attend to the ward's nutrition, clothing, shelter, and well-being. The guardian must make decisions regarding the ward's support, care, health, safety, rehabilitation, education, therapeutic treatment and, if not inconsistent with an order of commitment, the ward's residence.

The guardian can supervise the ward's routine medical care unless the ward objects, however, if there is a medical emergency, the guardian can supervise the ward's medical care even if he or she objects. If the ward refuses necessary medical treatment, the guardian can petition the court for the power to give informed consent for the ward.

If the ward is clearly unable to give informed consent, because of a stroke, dementia or some other problem that makes communication with the medical provider impossible, the medical provider will generally fill out a declaration for the guardian to submit to the court.

If the court approves the request, the guardian will be able to make most medical decisions without the court's permission. However, if the ward suffers from dementia and needs to be in a secure long-term care facility, or needs special drugs to treat the condition, the guardian must generally petition the court for permission to have the ward confined, or to administer necessary medication.

In order to receive special medical powers, the medical provider must complete an affidavit or declaration concerning the ward's condition, and the extent to which the ward can participate in his or her own medical decision-making. This document must be filed with the court.

A sample capacity declaration is set forth at Appendix 6.

The guardian may not revoke a Do Not Resuscitate Order, a Durable Power of Attorney for Health Care, or Living Will. However, a court is generally permitted to make any order relating to withdrawal of life-sustaining treatment, including artificial nutrition and hydration. Any application for such an order is usually made separate and apart from the guardianship proceeding itself because it is based upon other legal considerations.

THE GUARDIANSHIP PETITION

Filing the Petition

The guardianship proceeding is initiated by the filing of a petition for guardianship. The petition is generally in the form of a sworn statement by the petitioner alleging that the proposed ward is incapable of managing his or her personal affairs, and is in need of a guardian. The reason for guardianship set forth in the petition should conform to the actual diagnosis given in the medical report, and the basic statutory criteria that demonstrates the need for a guardianship.

Such criteria may include mental deterioration, physical incapacity, developmental disability, or mental illness and an inability to manage one's personal or financial affairs as a result. However, the fact that a person may be elderly, frail, developmentally disabled or mentally ill, without proof of an inability to manage his or her affairs, does not satisfy the statutory criteria.

Although the petitioner may petition for guardianship without the use of an attorney, the advice of legal counsel may be beneficial, particularly if there are complex personal or financial issues involved. In addition, an attorney can advise the petitioner whether there is sufficient evidence supporting the application for guardianship, and ensure that all of the statutory requirements and local rules are followed.

Eligible Petitioners

Any interested person or friend can file a petition to become a guardian. The usual order of preference is as follows:

1. Spouse;

2. Adult child;

3. Parent;

4. Sibling;

5. Any other person permitted by law to serve as a guardian; or

6. The Public Guardian if there is no suitable relative or friend able to serve as guardian. The Office of Public Guardian has personal guardians, conservators, and property administrators with experience serving in this capacity. There may be fees, however, fees are generally based on one's ability to pay.

Procedural Steps

Although specific procedural issues may differ according to jurisdiction, basically, the petitioner must:

1. Complete the guardianship petition;

2. File the petition with the appropriate court;

3. Provide notice of the petition and hearing date upon any interested individuals; and

4. Participate in the guardianship hearing.

Required Information

In order to complete the guardianship petition, the petitioner will generally need the following personal information about the proposed ward:

1. Full name;

2. Address;

3. Date of birth;

4. Social security number;

5. Contact information for the ward's medical providers, including name, address, phone and fax number, and medical record number.

Determining the Venue

Venue for a guardianship proceeding for an incapacitated person is in the county of the state in which the proposed ward resides and, if the proposed ward has been admitted to an institution by order of a court of competent jurisdiction, in the county in which the court is located.

Venue for the appointment of an emergency or a temporary substitute guardian of an incapacitated person is also in the county in which the proposed ward is present.

Notice Requirement

The petitioner must provide notice of his or her petition for guardianship and notice of the guardianship hearing within a certain number of days prior to the hearing date set by the court. Notice is accomplished by serving a copy of these papers upon certain individuals, which may include known relatives of the proposed ward, including:

1. Parents;

2. Grandparents;

3. Siblings;

4. Children;

5. Grandchildren; and

6. Spouse.

In addition, the proposed ward is also entitled to notice, along with the names and addresses of any previously appointed guardians or agents. Although friends of the proposed ward have no statutory right to notice, they should also be given the opportunity to be heard, in order to demonstrate to the court that every effort has been made to be thorough and fair.

Generally, a professional process server should be used to serve the papers, although most courts permit any person over the age of 18 to serve the papers. After the papers are served, the person who served the papers must complete an affidavit of service, which must be submitted to the court as proof of compliance with the notice requirement.

Withdrawing the Petition

Once the guardianship petition has been filed, it generally may not be dismissed or withdrawn without the court's permission. This is because the petitioner's sworn statement alleges that the proposed ward is incapacitated, unable to manage his or her personal or financial affairs, and, thus, needs the assistance of a guardian.

Courts do not like to dismiss a petition, or allow it to be withdrawn, unless it can be shown that there is a change of circumstances, such as a physician's report explaining why the guardianship is no longer necessary. Thus, before a guardianship petition is filed, the petitioner must make sure that the proposed ward meets the legal standard for guardianship.

THE GUARDIANSHIP INVESTIGATION

As part of the guardianship proceeding, the court may appoint a neutral investigator to provide information to the court. In addition, the court will also appoint a physician to evaluate the physical and mental condition of the proposed ward.

The investigator will meet with the petitioner and the proposed ward. When meeting with the proposed ward, the investigator will explain the guardianship proceeding and his or her rights, and discuss how guardianship will affect his or her life. If the proposed ward does not have the capacity to understand, the investigator will determine whether a lawyer should be appointed to represent his or her interests. The court will appoint an attorney for a proposed ward who cannot afford legal representation.

The investigator may also interview the proposed ward's family, friends and any other important persons who may have information that would assist the investigator in making his or her determination. The investigator will include his or her findings in a report to the court, along with his or her recommendations.

After the court appoints a guardian, the investigator generally reviews the case periodically to make sure the guardian is fulfilling his or her responsibilities and the ward's rights are being upheld. If the investigator is concerned that there is a problem, he or she may petition the court to remove the guardian and ask that a lawyer be appointed for the ward.

THE MEDICAL REPORT

The medical report forms the basis upon which the need for a guardianship is decided. Oftentimes, in uncontested cases, the medical provider who prepared the report does not have to testify. Therefore, the report itself is a major piece of evidence that is carefully scrutinized by the court in reaching its finding. A simple statement that a guardianship is necessary will not suffice.

In general, the medical report must include the following information:

1. The nature and type of disability, including the extent of the proposed ward's impairment;

2. The manner in which the disability affects the proposed ward's decision making capacity and ability to function independently;

3. An analysis of the proposed ward's mental and physical condition, and level of functioning; and

4. The medical provider's opinion concerning the proposed ward's need for a guardianship, and the type and scope of guardianship necessary.

In addition, the report must be recently made or updated, and should set forth the credentials and contact information for the medical provider who prepared the report.

THE GUARDIANSHIP HEARING

After the petition is filed and the investigation is completed, a hearing is held, at which time, the court hears all of the testimony and other evidence.

Contested Case

In a contested guardianship case, the proposed ward is entitled to procedural due process. For example, the court may appoint a guardian ad litem whose responsibility is to protect the rights and interests of the proposed ward. In addition, the court may appoint an attorney to represent the proposed ward.

In some jurisdictions, the proposed ward is entitled to have a jury determine the issue of disability after hearing all of the evidence. In addition, the proposed ward may request that the court appoint independent medical and psychiatric experts to refute the expert testimony presented by the petitioner.

The proposed ward is also entitled to: (1) appear at the guardianship hearing; (2) cross-examine witnesses; and (3) present evidence. The burden of proof lies with the petitioner to show that the proposed ward requires a guardian to manage his or her affairs. The standard of proof generally requires clear and convincing evidence.

Uncontested Case

In an uncontested case, the court will rely on the medical report, and may read the report into the court record. In many courts, a witness who is familiar with the proposed ward will testify about the proposed ward's need for guardianship.

After all of the evidence is introduced, the court will consider certain factors to make its ruling, including:

1. The nature and extent of the proposed ward's general intellectual and physical functioning;

2. The extent of the proposed ward's impairment;

3. The ability of the proposed ward to make responsible personal decisions;

4. The ability of the proposed ward to manage his or her personal and financial affairs;

5. The appropriateness of the proposed living arrangements; and

6. The impact of the disability on the proposed ward's ability to carry out daily living activities and make important decisions.

LETTERS OF GUARDIANSHIP

Upon conclusion of the hearing, the judge will consider all of the evidence supporting the petition for guardianship, as well as any opposition to the petition. If, after considering all of the evidence, the court determines that the person is legally incapacitated, a guardian is appointed to manage the ward's affairs.

The appointed guardian may be required to file an acceptance of the appointment with the court along with any required bond, however, if the guardian is appointed only "of the person," and not "of the estate," the court may waive the filing of the bond.

In addition, the court will issue letters of guardianship and an order for guardianship. Either a certified or authenticated copy of the letters of guardianship may serve as proof of authority by appointment.

Limitations

The court order appointing the guardian must be designed to accomplish the least restrictive form of intervention, and limited to only the necessary powers to deal with the ward's level of incapacity.

If the evidence indicates that the ward is incapable of handling his or her financial affairs, but quite capable of making day to day decisions on personal matters, the guardian's role may be limited to managing the ward's financial affairs, and the ward may retain the right to manage his or her own personal affairs.

Any limits on the powers of the guardian must be stated in the letters of guardianship. Third parties are charged with knowledge of the restrictions endorsed on the letters of guardianship, and are subject to possible liability for failing to act in accordance with those restrictions.

Appeal Rights

The court's decision may be appealed, and some states may suspend the appointment of a guardian until the appeal process is exhausted. In addition, the ward may petition for restoration of his or her rights upon a subsequent showing of competency.

LIMITED GUARDIANSHIP

A limited guardianship is a type of guardianship for people who are developmentally disabled. UGPPA provides for limited guardianships and conservatorships. A guardian or conservator obtains only the powers over the ward or protected person that are the least restrictive possible.

The court appoints an individual, known as a limited guardian, to care for the developmentally disabled adult ward. Generally, a person qualifies as developmentally disabled if he or she has an IQ of less than 70, or suffers from certain other disabling conditions.

The court determines the rights and responsibilities of the limited guardian, depending on the capabilities of the ward. Developmentally disabled individuals are often capable of carrying out many activities without any assistance, therefore, the court generally "limits" the guardian's powers. The guardian obtains only the powers that are the least restrictive possible. The objective is to provide maximum personal freedom from authority for the ward or protected person.

In general, a limited guardian has the power to:

1. Make decisions about where the ward will reside;

2. Review the ward's confidential records;

3. Sign a contract on behalf of the ward;

4. Withhold or give consent for medical treatment, including most medical procedures;

5. Arrange for the ward's education and vocational training; and

6. Manage the ward's financial affairs.

The limited guardian cannot use the ward's funds to pay him or herself a salary without a court order, however, the limited guardian may request that the court award compensation and costs at the time he or she files the annual report.

VOTING RIGHTS

A person age 18 or older has the right to vote, and there is no test to determine whether the voter is competent. However, those individuals for whom a full guardianship has been approved due to mental incapacity are generally not permitted to vote. If the guardianship is limited, the ward's right to vote depends on the language of the guardianship order.

It is the responsibility of each citizen, or the citizen's guardian, to know whether the ward is eligible to vote. Voting or registering to vote while ineligible is a class C felony punishable by imprisonment and/or a fine.

CHAPTER 4:
MENTAL HEALTH GUARDIANSHIP
AND CIVIL COMMITMENT

IN GENERAL

Millions of Americans suffer from mental illness. Unfortunately, many do not seek treatment for this serious health condition. Often, this is because they do not recognize that they are suffering from mental illness, and ignore their symptoms. For those who do recognize their condition, treatment may be administered on an outpatient basis. Treatment commonly includes counseling and medication.

A mental health guardianship is implemented for people who are seriously mentally ill and in need of special care. As with an ordinary guardianship, the court appoints an individual, known as the mental health guardian, to care for a mentally ill adult ward.

MENTAL ILLNESS

The mental health guardianship is only used for adults who suffer from a mental illness, such as a serious biological brain disorder, including:

1. Schizophrenia;

2. Bi-polar disorder (manic depressive);

3. Schizo-affective disorder;

4. Clinical depression; and

5. Obsessive compulsive disorder.

Individuals with organic brain disorders, brain trauma, retardation, alcohol or drug addiction, or dementia, are generally not eligible for a mental health guardianship.

In order for the court to approve a mental health guardianship, it must find, beyond a reasonable doubt, that the mentally ill person, is gravely disabled. Gravely disabled means that, because of a mental disorder, the person cannot take care of his or her basic needs, e.g., food, clothing, or shelter. This determination is generally made by a psychiatrist.

ROLE OF THE GUARDIAN

In general, the mental health guardian has the duty to take care of and protect the seriously mentally ill ward, and the power to handle the ward's financial matters. In addition, the guardian generally has the power to:

1. Give consent to mental health treatment, even if the ward objects;

2. Agree to the use of psychotropic drugs, although the ward may physically refuse to take the drugs;

3. Place the mentally ill ward in a locked facility provided a psychiatrist states that it is needed and the facility agrees, even if the ward objects;

4. Decide where the mentally ill ward will live when not confined to the locked facility; and

5. Manage the ward's financial affairs.

The guardian is obligated to act in the best interests of the mentally ill ward, and must have enough medical and social information to make those decisions.

CHALLENGING THE GUARDIANSHIP

Depending on the jurisdiction, the ward may be able to challenge the mental health guardianship by petitioning the court for a rehearing. At the rehearing, the ward has the burden of proving that he or she is not "gravely disabled," and can provide for his or her own food, clothing and shelter.

The petition should set forth details about how the ward plans on taking care of his or her needs. If another person will be assisting the ward by providing food, clothing and shelter, that person should write a letter to the court indicating his or her willingness to do so. The letter should accompany the petition. The petition should also explain how and where the ward will obtain any necessary medical or mental health treatment.

It is advisable to have a lawyer represent the ward at the rehearing. The lawyer who represented the ward in the initial proceeding would be a good choice insofar as he or she is familiar with the ward and the circumstances surrounding the mental health guardianship.

CIVIL COMMITMENT

When a mentally ill person refuses medical treatment for his or her condition, the symptoms may become so severe that he or she requires placement in a locked facility. The ward's mental health guardian, if one has been appointed, may petition the court to have that person confined.

In addition, if the individual engages in behavior that endangers the individual, or the public, law enforcement officers may transport that person to a hospital. At the hospital, the individual is examined by medical and mental health professionals to determine whether he or she should be hospitalized for a period of time. The hospital may then petition the court for civil commitment to involuntarily confine the individual so he or she can receive mental health treatment.

Civil commitment is the term used to refer to the surrender of a seriously mentally ill individual to the custody of an institution. Civil commitment involves an extraordinary constraint on one's personal liberty, and is often seen as a last resort when outpatient treatment is not a viable alternative. Thus, the state's interest in protecting the public as well as the individual must outweigh the individual's personal liberty interests.

The court's power of civil commitment is derived from the Tenth Amendment to the U.S. Constitution. The state's police power permits the government to protect people from harm to themselves or to others. The state also has the power to protect those people who do not have the capacity to care for themselves. This is known as "parens patriae."

Required Standard

The standard required for civil commitment varies from state to state, however, it generally requires that the individual is deemed so mentally ill or disabled that a danger exists to the individual, or to others, due to the mental illness or disability.

O'Connor v. Donaldson

In *O'Connor* v. *Donaldson*, 422 U.S. 563 (1975), the Supreme Court set forth a legal standard for civil commitment of people suffering from a mental illness. The respondent, Kenneth Donaldson, was civilly committed as a mental patient in the Florida State Hospital against his will for almost 15 years. Originally, his father had him committed because he claimed his son was suffering from delusions. He was diagnosed with paranoid schizophrenia, and admitted for treatment.

Donaldson repeatedly demanded his release throughout his confinement, claiming that he was not dangerous. His requests for release were supported by responsible persons willing to provide him any care he might need on release. Dr. O'Connor, superintendent of the facility, denied these requests.

In 1971, Donaldson brought an action against O'Connor and other members of the hospital staff, alleging that he was being intentionally and maliciously deprived of his constitutional right to liberty. A jury returned a verdict awarding damages to Donaldson, which was affirmed on appeal.

The U.S. Supreme Court granted O'Connor's petition for certiorari, agreeing to hear the case due to the important constitutional issues involved in civil commitment. The evidence showed that Donaldson's confinement was "a simple regime of enforced custodial care, not a program designed to alleviate or cure his supposed illness." Witnesses stated that Donaldson had received nothing but custodial care while in the facility. The jury found that petitioner did so confine respondent, and concluded that petitioner had violated respondent's right to liberty.

In a unanimous decision, the Supreme Court ruled that a state cannot constitutionally confine a non-dangerous individual who is capable of surviving safely in freedom by himself or with the help of willing and responsible family members or friend.

Addington v. Texas

In 1979, another civil commitment case worked its way, on appeal, to the U.S. Supreme Court. In *Addington* v. *Texas*, 441 U.S. 418 (1979), Appellant Addington's mother filed a petition for his indefinite commitment to a state mental hospital. Addington challenged his commitment. The state trial court instructed the jury to determine whether, based on "clear, unequivocal and convincing evidence," appellant was mentally ill and required hospitalization for his own welfare and protection or the protection of others.

The jury found that appellant was mentally ill and that he required hospitalization, and the trial court ordered his commitment for an indefinite period. On appeal, Addington argued that the trial court should have employed the "beyond a reasonable doubt" standard of proof. The Texas Court of Appeals reversed, agreeing with appellant on the standard of proof issue.

The Texas Supreme Court reversed the Court of Appeals' decision and reinstated the trial court's judgment, concluding that a "preponderance of the evidence" standard of proof in a civil commitment proceeding satisfied due process, and that, since the trial court's improper instructions in the instant case had benefited appellant, the error was harmless.

The U.S. Supreme Court granted certiorari and heard Addington's appeal. After considering the evidence, the Supreme Court ruled that a "clear and convincing" standard of proof is required by the Fourteenth Amendment in a civil proceeding brought under state law to involuntarily commit an individual to a state mental hospital for an indefinite period of time.

Civil Commitment Procedure

The procedure for civil commitment depends on the jurisdiction. Generally, the commitment proceeding is similar to the guardianship proceeding discussed above, as follows:

1. A petition is filed by the state or another interested party;

2. Notice is given to the individual and any other interested parties; and

3. A hearing is scheduled.

An attorney will be appointed for anyone who cannot afford legal representation. In addition, an investigation by a psychiatrist or psychologist to assess the individual's mental state will be undertaken.

If no alternatives to commitment can be found, a formal hearing is held, usually before a judge. The petitioner presents his or her case, which must satisfy the burden of proof. In 1979, the Supreme Court held that the standard of proof in a civil commitment proceeding must be by "clear and convincing evidence," so as to protect the due process rights of the mentally ill. Generally, the evidence introduced at the hearing consists of expert testimony from the individual's treating psychiatrist.

If it is determined that the individual should be or remain confined, that decision may be appealed. During confinement, the individual's condition is reviewed periodically to determine whether continued confinement is necessary.

Challenging Confinement

If a rehearing is unsuccessful, depending on the jurisdiction, the ward may be able to file a petition for a writ of habeas corpus, asking the court to find that his or her confinement is unlawful. If the court agrees, it will issue a writ of habeas corpus. Alternatively, the court can schedule an evidentiary hearing, or simply deny the petition for a writ.

If the ward is unsuccessful in fighting confinement, he or she can ask the guardian for a less restrictive placement. It is helpful to have the staff at the facility support the request with a favorable recommendation.

CHAPTER 5:
STANDBY GUARDIANSHIP

IN GENERAL

Traditional guardianship has historically been used to provide for the care of a child in the event of the parent's death or permanent disability, and is generally regarded as a permanent transfer of custody and authority from the parent to the guardian.

One of the more recent approaches to transferring custody is facilitated through standby guardian laws, which allow the parent to continue his or her parental relationship with the child while the parent is still living. This mechanism is also available to the spouse of an incapacitated person, or the parent of an adult disabled child.

Standby guardianship laws allow parents to plan for their children's future in case the parents should die prematurely or become incapacitated. These laws are intended to fill the gap between the child's life with the disabled parent and life following the parent's death, and help make this transition easier.

Although a minority of states have always had laws that allow parents to designate "standby" guardians, the need for such laws became apparent when serious, debilitating, and potentially fatal diseases, such as AIDS, began impacting families with minor children on a broader scale.

The purpose of standby guardianship is to allow a parent, who may be suffering from a chronic or terminal illness, to pre-arrange for the care and custody of his or her children if it becomes necessary at some future date.

Before the availability of standby guardianship, a terminally ill parent did not have many legal options when trying to plan for the future care of his or her children. For example, although a will may designate a guardian for the minor children, as set forth in Chapter 6, "Conservatorship: Protecting the Property of the Ward," such a provision does not take effect until the death of the parent.

Transferring guardianship of the child, e.g., to social services for foster care placement or adoption, is not a good option because it requires the parent to immediately relinquish the child to a third party. In addition, informal arrangements are inadequate in that the caregivers do not have any legal rights, therefore, problems may arise in obtaining medical care, enrolling the children in school, obtaining benefits for the children, etc.

Standby guardianship bridges the gap by providing for the voluntary transfer of the child's custody to the appointed guardian upon the parent's incapacity, while allowing the parent to retain parental rights and shared decision-making authority over the child. Permanent guardianship is not established until the parent passes away.

Thousands of children are orphaned each year as a result of the death of a parent, thus, there is a serious need for standby guardianship. Allowing the parent to plan for the child's care and custody while the parent is still relatively healthy provides some assurance that the child will be placed in a stable, safe, and permanent home when it becomes necessary.

STATE STANDBY GUARDIANSHIP LAWS

Approximately 21 states and the District of Columbia have made statutory provisions for standby guardianships. Although there are differences among the states, most of the current standby guardianship laws have several components in common:

1. A parent may designate a certain person to be the standby guardian for his or her minor children.

2. The guardianship may go into effect during the parent's lifetime and may continue in effect after the parent's death.

3. The parent retains a large degree of control over the guardianship. He or she may determine when it can begin, although guardianship transfer may commence automatically if the parent becomes seriously ill or mentally incapacitated.

4. The parent shares decision-making responsibility with the guardian. During the parent's lifetime, the guardian is expected to be in the background, undertake responsibility when needed, and step back when the parent is feeling well.

5. The order for standby guardianship must be supported by the authority of a court that has examined facts relevant to the particular family.

6. The events that trigger the activation of the standby guardian include the death or the incapacity of the parent or legal guardian. Some states also allow the parent to consent to a transfer of guardianship at any time the parent feels it is appropriate.

7. The statutes allow the parent to revoke the standby guardian agreement at any time.

Many states allow a parent or legal guardian to designate a standby guardian regardless of the parent's health status. However, some states preclude such a designation unless the parent is at significant risk of death or incapacity within a specified time period. Further, some states require a documented health status report by an attending physician to initiate the court process.

ESTABLISHING THE STANDBY GUARDIANSHIP

A standby guardian for a minor child is an individual who has been voluntarily named by a parent to become the legal guardian of his or her minor children if the parent becomes unable to care for the children. It is important to note that the parents have the right to designate a person of their own choosing to take on this role.

Standby guardianship is typically established by (1) petition; or (2) written designation. The difference between these two options is that the petition process allows the parent to formally plan for the care and custody of his or her child before becoming incapacitated, whereas the designation process is carried out privately, and the burden is on the standby guardian to notify the court after the child's parent becomes incapacitated and dies.

Petition

A standby guardianship may be established by filing a petition for judicial appointment of the standby guardian, followed by a court hearing regarding the petition. The petition is filed prior to the event that necessitates the standby guardianship—i.e, the "triggering event."

A sample petition for standby guardianship is set forth at Appendix 7.

Written Designation

A standby guardianship may be established by written designation. After the death or incapacity of the parent or legal guardian, the designated standby guardian must notify the court of the triggering event, file a petition for guardianship, and participate in a court hearing to be appointed legal guardian.

The designation document generally includes the following statements:

1. That the parent is qualified to establish a standby guardianship because he or she has a terminal or chronic illness;

2. That the standby guardianship becomes active when a "triggering event" occurs;

3. That the triggering event is mental incapacity, physical disability, or death of the parent; and

4. That the parent's consent governs all aspects of the guardianship while the parent is still capable of giving consent.

Some states have a statutory designate form that the parent may use. Most statutes generally require that parents sign the form before two witnesses so as to avoid forgery.

ACTIVATING THE STANDBY GUARDIAN'S AUTHORITY

In order to activate the standby guardian's authority, a "triggering event" must occur first. Events that may trigger the appointment of the standby guardian include:

1. The death of the parent;

2. The mental or physical incapacitation of the parent such that he or she is unable to care for the children; or

3. Upon the parent's request.

As previously stated, many states also mandate that an attending physician document the parent's incapacity or debilitation.

Typically, upon a triggering event, the standby guardian has a statutorily prescribed amount of time in which to file confirming documents and/or a petition for approval. The standby guardian must obtain evidence to submit to the court, which may include the medical provider's determination of incapacitation, the parent's consent, and/or a death certificate, etc.

The evidence must be submitted to the court within a certain number of days following the triggering event in order to activate the guardianship. Under the designation process described above, the standby guardian must also file a petition for appointment as guardian for the minor child.

Standby guardians must also generally petition for permanent guardianship or initiate custody proceedings within a specified time period.

State statutes vary significantly with respect to activation of the standby guardian's authority, and should be consulted and carefully followed.

THE COURT HEARING

The guardianship cannot be confirmed until the triggering event has occurred and the evidence has been filed with the court. If the parent's physical or mental incapacity is the triggering event, a physician's statement is required to be filed as part of the evidence. The guardianship does not become effective until the court makes a finding that the guardianship is in the best interests of the child.

Although the parent is allowed to name their choice for guardian, the court must still examine all of the factors and decide whether the parent's choice is appropriate. Some states provide for the appointment of a guardian ad litem or attorney for the child to assist the judge in making this decision.

The court will base its findings on the declarations in the designating document and the petition for standby guardianship. Nevertheless, unless there is compelling evidence against the named guardian, the parent's choice will generally be given great deference by the court.

Generally, a hearing will be scheduled whether or not the petition is uncontested. Notice is required to be given to the parent. The parent is not required to attend the hearing, e.g., if he or she is too sick to appear. In several states, a hearing is not held unless required, e.g., if the non-custodial parent contests the appointment of a standby guardian. Many states also provide that a child of a certain age must be notified and that the court must consider the child's preferences. The age requirement varies by state.

After the parent dies, the standby guardianship is generally converted into a permanent guardianship. In some states, this requires the filing of a separate petition to the court to finalize the permanent guardianship. In some states, the petition must be filed within a certain number of days following the triggering event.

RIGHTS OF THE NON-CUSTODIAL PARENT

States laws vary with respect to the involvement of the non-custodial parent when it comes to appointing a standby guardian. Some states require the consent of both parents, where the non-custodial parent has parental rights.

Notice Requirement

Unless the non-custodial parent's rights have been terminated, all of the states require that the non-custodial parent be given notice of the standby guardian proceedings. Termination of parental rights may occur, e.g., if a court has found that the non-custodial parent is not willing, fit or able to take on a parenting role for the child. Notice must occur either at the initial court approval or when the standby guardian provides proof of a triggering event and requests legal guardianship.

Several states require that the custodial parent make a "diligent effort" to locate the non-custodial parent, while some states simply require that the custodial parent make a "reasonable effort" to find and serve notice upon the non-custodial parent. The "reasonable effort" standard may be satisfied by mailing and attempting personal service of the notice to the non-custodial parent's last known address, or by publishing notice of the proceeding in the newspaper.

A few states have even less stringent requirements. For example, in New York, notice is only required to be given to the non-custodial parent if:

(1) he or she resides in New York;

(2) his or her address is known; and

(3) he or she has not been deprived of guardianship rights by a court.

MAINTAINING PARENTAL AUTHORITY

State laws vary with respect to the relationship between the authority of the parent and that of the standby guardian. An important component of standby guardianship is joint decision-making afforded the guardian and the parent. Thus, most states provide that once standby guardianship is activated, the standby guardian and living parent have concurrent authority, and that the commencement of a guardianship does not in any way limit the parent's parental rights.

Nevertheless, a few states provide that once the standby guardianship is activated, the standby guardian assumes sole authority. Some states also provide that a standby guardian's authority is inactive if and when the parent becomes healthy and able to care for the child again. If so, the attending physician's written certification of the parent's improved medical status may be required.

REVOKING THE STANDBY GUARDIANSHIP

Once the guardianship becomes permanent, unless it is revoked or rescinded, it continues until the child turns 18, or until there is another event, such as emancipation, marriage, enlistment in the armed services, etc.

States laws vary with respect to withdrawal of standby guardianship. In most states, when an appointment has been made by written designation, the parent may revoke the designation by written notice to the standby guardian.

However, if the standby guardian's appointment has been approved by the court, most states generally require that written revocation be filed with the court and that the standby guardian be notified in writing. Some states do not have any laws regarding withdrawal. In addition, the standby guardian may refuse an appointment by notifying the parent in writing.

THE UNIFORM GUARDIANSHIP AND PROTECTIVE PROCEEDINGS ACT

The complexity and non-uniformity of state standby guardianship laws make it difficult to implement, and questionable whether this vehicle will be widely used in the future. Section 202 of the Uniform Guardianship and Protective Proceedings Act sets forth a more simplified statute that states could adopt, in whole or in part:

Section 202. Parental Appointment of Guardian.

(a) A guardian may be appointed by will or other signed writing by a parent for any minor child the parent has or may have in the future. The appointment may specify the desired limitations on the powers to be given to the guardian. The appointing parent may revoke or amend the appointment before confirmation by the court.

(b) Upon petition of an appointing parent and a finding that the appointing parent will likely become unable to care for the child within [two] years, and after notice as provided in Section 205(a), the court, before the appointment becomes effective, may confirm the parent's selection of a guardian and terminate the rights of others to object.

(c) Subject to Section 203, the appointment of a guardian becomes effective upon the appointing parent's death, an adjudication that the parent is an incapacitated person, or a written determination by a physician who has examined the parent that the parent is no longer able to care for the child, whichever first occurs.

(d) The guardian becomes eligible to act upon the filing of an acceptance of appointment, which must be filed within 30 days after the guardian's appointment becomes effective. The guardian shall: (1) file the acceptance of appointment and a copy of the will with the court of the [county] in which the will was or could be probated or, in the case of another appointing instrument,

CHAPTER 6:
CONSERVATORSHIP: PROTECTING
THE PROPERTY OF THE WARD

IN GENERAL

If a person becomes incapacitated, he or she may need someone to handle financial matters and manage his or her assets and property. The individual who is appointed guardian of a minor or incapacitated adult does not automatically become conservator of the ward's estate. The prospective conservator must petition the court for this appointment. This petition can be filed at the same time a petition for guardianship is filed, or it can be filed at a later date. Once a conservatorship is established, the ward is known as a conservatee in that proceeding.

If a petition for guardianship and a petition for conservatorship for the same person are commenced or pending in the same court, the two petitions can generally be consolidated, and heard and decided by the court at the same time.

THE ROLE OF THE CONSERVATOR

Fiduciary Role

The prospective conservator must carefully consider whether he or she will be able to fulfill the responsibilities associated with acting as conservator. The conservator who is appointed to manage the financial affairs of the conservatee serves as a fiduciary to the conservatee.

A fiduciary is one who stands in a relationship of trust to another and must act prudently and in the best interests of the person for whom he or she is appointed as a fiduciary. Therefore, the law provides for strict reporting requirements.

For example, the conservator is generally required to file periodic accountings on the conservatee's income, property, and the disbursements from the estate. Further, the court may require the conservator to obtain permission before making any major financial decisions affecting the estate.

Costs and Expenses

Conservatorships can be time-consuming and costly. For example, a conservator is required to attend court hearings, consult with accountants and lawyers, and keep up with the detailed paperwork that must be filed on a regular basis.

The conservator may also be required to post a bond to protect the estate in case of negligent mismanagement or waste of the estate proceeds. A bond is a type of insurance policy designed to protect the conservatee's estate. Insofar as bond premiums are paid from the conservatee's assets, it is preferable that the conservator be competent so as to avoid this expense.

Public or professional conservators are reimbursed for their expenses and compensated for their services from the conservatee's assets. The court must generally approve these payments, provided they are reasonable. A relative generally serves as conservator without compensation, however, he or she may petition the court for compensation.

QUALIFICATIONS

The following persons and/or entities are generally qualified to serve as conservators:

1. Any natural person who is of full age is qualified to be a conservator provided he or she is mentally competent and has not been declared unsuitable by a court;

2. Banks and trust companies;

3. Private nonprofit corporations.

For children, preference is given to a parent provided he or she is qualified and suitable. Otherwise, it is up to the court to appoint a qualified, suitable individual who is willing to serve as conservator.

DUTIES OF THE CONSERVATOR

The money and other assets of the conservatee are called the "estate."' Once appointed, the conservator of the estate handles the conservatee's financial matters. The conservator is required to manage the funds; collect and make an inventory of the assets; keep accurate financial records; and regularly file financial accountings with the court. However, the conservator is not obligated to support the conservatee.

Nevertheless, the conservator does have the responsibility to make sure the conservatee receives all of the benefits to which he or she is entitled. This may include social security and veterans' benefits, public assistance, disability benefits, pension benefits, and health care coverage.

The conservator cannot make medical decisions for the conservatee. This responsibility rests with the "guardian of the person," or the individual named in the conservatee's durable power of attorney for health care.

As further discussed below, it is the duty of the conservator of the estate to:

(1) Manage, protect, and preserve the estate;

(2) Invest the estate prudently;

(3) Keep an accounting of the estate; and

(4) Perform all duties required of the conservator by law.

Manage the Estate

Make Prudent Investments

The conservator must manage the estate assets with the care of a prudent person dealing with someone else's property. This means the conservator must be cautious and may not make speculative or risky investments.

Keep Estate Assets Separate

The conservator must keep the money and property of the estate separate from everyone else's, including their own. When a bank account is opened for the estate, the account name must indicate that it is a conservatorship account and not the conservator's personal account.

The conservator should use the conservatee's social security number when opening estate accounts, and should never deposit estate funds in his or her personal account or otherwise mix them with his or her own funds or anyone else's funds, even for brief periods. Securities in the estate must be held in a name that shows that they are estate property and not the conservator's personal property.

Interest-Bearing Accounts

Estate funds should be placed in interest-bearing accounts, except for checking accounts used for ordinary expenses. The conservator may deposit estate funds in insured accounts in federally insured financial institutions, but should not put more than $100,000 in any single institution. The conservator should consult with an attorney before making other kinds of investments.

Blocked Accounts

A blocked account is an account with a financial institution in which money is placed. No person may withdraw funds from a blocked account without the court's permission. Depending on the amount and character of the property, the conservator may elect, or the court may require, that estate assets be placed in a blocked account. The conservator must follow the directions of the court and the procedures required to deposit funds in this type of account. The use of a blocked account is a safeguard and may save the estate the cost of a bond.

Miscellaneous Restrictions

The conservator will have many other restrictions on his or her authority to deal with estate assets. Without prior court order, the conservator may take fees or pay fees to his or her attorney. The conservator may not make a gift of estate assets to anyone, or borrow money from the estate. The conservator may not use estate funds to purchase real property without a prior court order.

If the conservator does not obtain the court's permission to spend estate funds, he or she may be compelled to reimburse the estate from his or her own personal funds and may be removed as conservator.

The conservator should consult with an attorney concerning the legal requirements relating to sales, leases, mortgages, and investment of estate property. If the conservatee of whose estate you are supervising has a living parent, or if that child receives assets or is entitled to support from another source, the conservator must obtain court approval before using conservatorship assets for the support, maintenance, or education of the conservatee.

The conservator must file a petition or include a request for approval in the original petition, and set forth which exceptional circumstances justify any use of conservatorship assets for the conservatee's support. The court will ordinarily grant such a petition for only a limited period of time, usually not to exceed one year, and only for specific and limited purposes.

Inventory the Estate

Locate Estate Property

The conservator must locate, take possession of, and protect the income and assets that will be administered in the estate. The conservator must also change the ownership of all assets into the conservatorship estate's name. For real estate, the conservator should record a copy of his or her Letters of Conservatorship with the county recorder in each county where the estate owns real property.

Determine Value of Estate

The conservator must arrange to have a court-appointed referee determine the value of the estate property unless the appointment is waived by the court. The conservator—not the referee—must determine the value of certain "cash items."

File Inventory and Appraisal

The conservator must file an inventory and appraisal within 90 days after appointment. He or she may be required to return to court 90 days after appointment to ensure that he or she has properly filed the inventory and appraisal.

Obtain Insurance Coverage

The conservator should make sure that there is appropriate and sufficient insurance covering the assets and risks of the estate. The insurance should be maintained in force throughout the entire period of the conservatorship or until the insured asset is sold.

Record Keeping

The conservator must keep complete, accurate records of each financial transaction affecting the estate. The checkbook for the conservatorship checking account is essential for keeping records of income and expenditures. The conservator should also keep receipts for all purchases.

Record keeping is critical because the conservator will have to prepare an accounting of all money and property that has been received, what has been spent, the date of each transaction, and its purpose. The conservator will also have to be able to describe in detail what was left after the estate's expenses were paid.

Accounting

The conservator must file a petition requesting that the court review and approve the accounting one year after appointment, and at least every two years after that. The court may ask the conservator to justify some or all expenditures. Thus, it is important to keep receipts and other documents available for the court's review, if requested.

If the conservator does not file their accounting as required, the court will order them to do so, and may remove the conservator for failure to file an accounting. The conservator must comply with all state and local rules when filing their accounting, and should check local rules for any special local requirements.

POWERS OF THE CONSERVATOR

Without a Court Order

Without a court order, the conservator generally has the power to:

1. Collect, receive, receipt for any principal or income;

2. Enforce, defend against or prosecute any claim against the conservatee or conservator;

3. Sue on, or defend claims in favor of, or against, the conservatee or conservator;

4. Sell or transfer personal property of a perishable nature, and personal property for which there is a regularly established market;

5. Vote at corporate meetings in person or by proxy;

6. Receive additional property from any source; and

7. Continue to hold any investment or other property originally received by the conservator.

With a Court Order

With a court order, the conservator generally has the power to:

1. Invest the funds belonging to the conservatee;

2. Execute leases;

3. Make payments to, and for the benefit of, the conservatee in any of the following ways:

(a) Directly to the conservatee;

(b) Directly for the maintenance, welfare and education of the conservatee;

(c) To the legal guardian of the person of the conservatee;

(d) To anyone who at the time shall have the custody and care of the person of the conservatee;

(e) In support of any person for whose support the conservatee is legally liable;

(f) To compromise or settle any claim by, or against, the conservatee or the conservator; and to adjust, arbitrate or compromise claims in favor or against the conservatee or conservator;

(g) To make an election for the conservatee who is a surviving spouse; and

(h) To do any other thing the court determines to be in the best interests of the conservatee and the conservatee's estate.

Estate Planning

Although the conservator of the estate has the ability to control the conservatee's finances, the conservatee still has the power to make a will, trust, or other estate-planning device. Under the following circumstances, however, the court will allow the conservator of the estate to undertake estate planning for the conservatee:

1. The conservatee is too sick to make a will, a trust or other estate planning device; or

2. The conservatorship was established because someone was taking advantage of the conservatee or exerting undue influence over him or her.

The Court may also authorize the conservator to change or revoke a trust, change insurance policies or annuities, and/or sign contracts on behalf of the conservatee. However, it is important that the conservator demonstrate to the court that, if the conservatee could act for him or herself, and could act as a reasonable person, the conservatee would want to make the requested changes.

THE CONSERVATORSHIP PETITION

Filing the Petition

The conservatorship proceeding is initiated by the filing of a petition. When petitioning for conservatorship, the prospective conservator must present evidence demonstrating how the proposed conservatee cannot manage his or her finances, or is easily influenced. The petition should set forth examples of events that have happened to support the claims, and identify others who are aware of the proposed conservatee's problems.

The petition must also list the proposed conservatee's assets in as much detail as possible, including information concerning bank accounts, brokerage accounts, stocks, savings bonds, cars, boats, real property, etc. The court will want to know how much the proposed conservatee's assets are worth, and how much income the proposed conservatee is entitled to receive each month.

A sample petition for the appointment of a conservator is set forth at Appendix 8.

Determining the Venue

Venue for a conservatorship proceeding is in the county of the state in which the proposed conservatee resides, whether or not a guardian has been appointed in another jurisdiction. If the proposed conservatee does not reside in the same state where the property is located, venue is generally in any county of the state where the proposed conservatee's property is located.

Notice Requirement

The petitioner must provide notice of his or her petition for conservatorship and the notice of hearing by serving a copy of these papers on certain individuals.

Petition to Appoint Temporary Conservator

A prospective conservator cannot petition the court for substituted judgment at the same time as the hearing to appoint a conservator is pending. However, if the proposed conservatee may be dying, and quick action is needed to protect the conservatee's estate, the prospective conservator may ask the court to consider a petition for appointment of a temporary conservator while the proceeding to appoint a permanent conservator proceeds.

A sample petition to appoint a temporary conservator is set forth at Appendix 9.

In this case, the court may issue letters and an order for a temporary conservatorship.

Sample letters of temporary conservatorship and an order appointing a temporary conservator are set forth at Appendix 10 and 11, respectively.

THE CONSERVATORSHIP HEARING

After a conservatorship petition is filed, the court considers the evidence presented to determine whether a conservator is necessary. If so, the court will generally appoint a family member, e.g., the spouse or adult child.

If several persons file a petition to be appointed conservator, the court must generally consider the petitions according to the preferences established by state law. For example, preference is generally given first to the conservatee's spouse, followed by registered domestic partner, adult children, adult siblings, or other blood relatives. If there is evidence of the proposed conservatee's choice in case a conservator was required, the court will take this under careful consideration.

However, the court is not bound by these preferences, and may appoint whomever the judge believes will best serve the estate. Although it is most likely that a relative will be appointed, the court may appoint a public conservator if there are no suitable relatives available to take on this responsibility.

Objections to the conservatorship, or the prospective conservator, may be filed by the proposed conservatee, family members, or any interested persons. The objection must be filed in court, and all interested persons must receive notice of the date on which the objection will be heard by the court.

LETTERS OF CONSERVATORSHIP

After considering all of the evidence, the court will determine whether a conservatorship is warranted. If so, the court will issue letters of conservatorship and an order appointing a conservator. The conservator may be required to file an acceptance of the appointment with the court along with any required bond.

Either a certified or authenticated copy of the letters of conservatorship may serve as proof of authority by appointment.

Sample letters of conservatorship and an order appointing a conservator are set forth at Appendix 12 and 13, respectively.

Appeal Rights

The court's decision may be appealed, and some states may suspend the appointment of a conservator until the appeal process is exhausted. In addition, the conservatee may petition for restoration of his or her rights upon a subsequent showing of competency.

Limitations

Any limits on the powers of the conservator must be stated in the letters of conservatorship. Third parties are charged with knowledge of the restrictions endorsed on the letters of conservatorship, and are subject to possible liability for failing to act in accordance with those restrictions.

ENDING THE CONSERVATORSHIP

The conservator is generally required to continue to act in this capacity until the court issues an order ending the conservatorship. This generally occurs under the following circumstances:

1. The death of the conservatee;

2. Improvement of the conservatee's medical condition such that he or she is able to manage his of her own financial affairs; or

3. There are no assets left in the conservatee's estate to manage.

Further, a conservator may be removed for the following reasons:

1. Failure to qualify as a fiduciary;

2. Mismanagement of the conservatee's estate; or

3. Failure to perform any duty.

A conservator may also resign. However, if the conservator resigns, the conservatorship continues, and another person is appointed to serve as conservator.

In addition, at the termination of the conservatorship, it is the duty of the conservator to deliver the assets of the conservatee to the person entitled to receive those assets.

CHAPTER 7:
ALTERNATIVES TO GUARDIANSHIP
AND CONSERVATORSHIP

IN GENERAL

Going through a guardianship/conservatorship proceeding can be a very traumatic experience, particularly for family members. Therefore, if a person plans ahead and executes documents to deal with the possibility of future incapacity or death, this will help to avoid such proceedings and ease the burden on family members. A guardian or a conservator should be appointed only if there are no other lesser restrictive alternatives that will meet the needs of the minor or incapacitated adult.

It is often mistakenly assumed that planning for incapacity is a topic reserved for the elderly, however, one should be aware that incapacity can occur at any time to any person, e.g., due to a tragic accident. Thus, every individual should consider executing the documents discussed in this chapter.

Alternatives to guardianship include the following:

1. Will provision appointing a guardian for a minor child;

2. A Living Will;

3. A Durable Power of Attorney for Health Care; and

4. A Durable Power of Attorney.

If, for any reason, the above-described alternatives to guardianship and conservatorship are unable to be used, an individual may also consider establishing a trust or executing a declaration designating a guardian in advance of incapacity, a procedure known as "standby guardianship."

Standby guardianship is discussed more fully in Chapter 5, "Standby Guardianship," of this Almanac.

The individual who considers using any of the documents described in this chapter must be of sound mind at the time the documents are executed or the documents will not be valid.

WILL PROVISION APPOINTING A GUARDIAN FOR A MINOR CHILD

If a decedent has a minor child at the time of death, the child is usually placed in, or remains in, the custody of the surviving parent. If both parents die simultaneously or if the surviving parent dies or is incapable of caring for the child, he or she must be placed in the custody of another responsible adult—a guardian.

If the parents did not execute a will that names a guardian for the minor child, a petition for guardianship must be filed, and a guardianship proceeding must be held, so that the court can appoint a guardian for the child, as discussed in Chapter 2, "Guardianship of a Minor," of this Almanac.

To avoid having someone appointed as guardian for your minor child who is undesirable, a provision in one's will should name the individual the decedent wishes to fulfill the role of guardian of his or her minor child upon his or her death. Although the decedent is free to name whoever he or she desires, the decedent's choice generally requires court approval unless, of course, it is the surviving parent.

In most cases, the court will abide by the decedent's wishes, unless there is a question of the designated person's fitness or someone contests the designation. The will may also name an alternate person to act as guardian, in the event the first choice for guardian is unavailable, unwilling, or unable to serve at the time of the decedent's death.

If the decedent leaves property to a minor child, any substantial gift must be supervised by an adult conservator, who may be named in the decedent's will. In most cases, the decedent simply names his or her surviving spouse. If there is no surviving spouse, the person who has been designated in the decedent's will as the personal guardian to take custody of the child may also act as the conservator for the child's property.

The conservator is obligated to use the money to provide for the needs of the child, and is required to regularly report to the court on how the money is being spent. In addition, the conservator generally needs permission from the court before investing the child's property. When the child reaches the age of majority, the conservatorship relationship automatically ends and the child is entitled to receive the remainder of his or her property.

A sample will provision appointing a guardian for a minor is set forth at Appendix 14.

THE LIVING WILL

A living will—also referred to as a directive to physicians—is a written declaration, directed to your physician, stating that you wish to forgo extraordinary treatment of a terminal illness, in order to die a natural death. A living will differs from an ordinary will in that a living will only specifies health care wishes whereas an ordinary will deals with the disposition of property upon your death.

Although living wills may not be statutorily recognized in all states, all 50 states and the District of Columbia have enacted laws providing for some type of living will, medical proxy, or health care durable power of attorney that governs the right of the patient, or the patient's designated representative, to make decisions about the patient's health care. Further, an individual has a constitutional right to execute a living will.

A sample living will is set forth at Appendix 15 of this Almanac, and a table of state living will statutes is set forth in Appendix 16.

Purpose

The purpose of a living will is to give a person the right to decide the manner in which he or she will be treated should they develop an incurable illness or enter a persistent vegetative state, and become unable to communicate their wishes at that time. Generally, a living will provides that no heroic measures should be taken to prolong the individual's life where there is no reasonable expectation of recovery. However, pain medication is still usually administered.

A living will also provides family and loved ones some guidance in making a very painful decision. Further, a living will allows a health care provider to withdraw or withhold life-support treatment without risking a medical malpractice lawsuit.

Requirements

There are certain requirements that must be met to ensure recognition of a living will.

Competency

Any adult over the age of 18 may execute a living will provided he or she is deemed to be competent, and acting of his or her own free will.

If the individual is incapacitated at the time of the decision to provide, withhold, or withdraw life-sustaining treatment or artificially provided nutrition and hydration, a living will is generally presumed to be valid. In the case of a minor, the minor's parents are generally relied upon by health-care providers as substitutes for the minor.

Diagnosis

In general, most states require that two physicians must diagnose the patient as terminally ill. Some states also provide that a living will is valid only if signed after the physician has informed the patient that he or she has an incurable illness. Before executing a living will, it is prudent to determine exactly what requirements are imposed in your state.

Form

A living will must be made in writing. There are many different living will forms available. There are official forms set forth in the living will statutes of many states, and unofficial forms created by state medical and bar associations, senior citizens' groups, and national right to die organizations, etc. Some states require the use of the statutory form for a living will to be valid.

Witnesses

A living will must be signed by the person executing the document, known as the "maker." Although state laws vary, living will statutes generally require that there be two witnesses to the maker's signature, neither of whom can be related to the maker or beneficiaries of his or her estate.

Medical Condition

A living will sets forth the medical condition under which the will would need to be consulted. Typical clauses read as follows:

1. If at any time I should have a terminal or incurable condition caused by injury, disease, or illness, certified to be terminal or incurable by at least two physicians, which within reasonable medical judgment would cause my death, and where the application of life-sustaining procedures would serve only to artificially prolong the moment of my death, I direct that such procedures be withheld or withdrawn, and that I be permitted to die with dignity.

2. If at any time I experience irreversible brain injury, or a disease, illness, or condition that results in my being in a permanent, irreversible vegetative or comatose state, and such injury, disease, illness, or condition would preclude any cognitive, meaningful, or functional future existence, I direct my physicians and any other attending

nursing or health care personnel to allow me to die with dignity, even if that requires the withdrawal or withholding of nutrition or hydration and my death will follow such withdrawal or withholding.

Life-Sustaining Treatment

A typical living will sets forth the type of life-sustaining treatment that may be provided, withheld or withdrawn. Basically, there are three general choices you can make regarding life-sustaining measures. You can request that:

1. Your health care providers do everything within their power to keep you alive;

2. The only life-sustaining measures you desire are nutrition (food) and hydration (water);

3. All artificial life-sustaining treatment is withheld, including nutrition and hydration.

Although it is not necessary to include every possible procedure to be provided, most living wills contain a clause setting forth the individual's intentions as to whether or not a certain "life-sustaining procedure" should be provided, withheld, or withdrawn if the individual's medical condition deteriorates. A typical clause reads as follows:

It is my expressed intent that the term "life-sustaining procedures" shall include not only medical or surgical procedures or interventions that utilize mechanical or other artificial means to sustain, restore, or supplant a vital function, but also shall include the placement, withdrawal, withholding, or maintenance of nasogastric tubes, gastrostomy, intravenous lines, heart-lung resuscitation, antibiotics, kidney dialysis, chemotherapy, or any other artificial, surgical, or invasive means for nutritional support and/or hydration.

Pain medication, nutrition and hydration are still usually given unless the living will specifically states that such treatment should be withheld.

Pregnancy Exclusions

Many living will statutes contain a pregnancy exclusion that provides that life-sustaining measures will continue regardless of any directive to the contrary until the pregnancy is complete, and that the pregnancy automatically invalidates the advance directive. For example, Missouri's law states:

"[T]he declaration to withdraw or withhold treatment by a patient diagnosed as pregnant by the attending physician shall have no effect during the course of the declarant's pregnancy." [Missouri Revised Statutes §49.025]

Other states use a viability standard to determine the enforceability of the advance directive. For example, Colorado's law states:

"In the case of a declaration of a qualified patient known to the attending physician to be pregnant, a medical evaluation shall be made as to whether the fetus is viable and could with a reasonable degree of medical certainty develop to live birth with continued application of life-sustaining procedures. If such is the case, the declaration shall be given no force or effect." [Colorado Medical Treatment Decision Act §15-18-104(2)].

A number of states are silent on the issue of pregnancy as it relates to a declaration contained in a living will. When a statute is silent, a court may be asked to decide whether the terms of the patient's living will would override the pregnancy. The court may hear testimony on this issue consisting of a patient's prior statements and conversations, to make its determination.

Amending or Revoking Your Living Will

As with any advance health care directive, you can amend your living will at any time, provided you are of sound mind and acting of your own free will. You may also revoke or terminate an existing living will without creating a new one.

If you choose to amend your living will, and the changes you wish to make are minor, you should put the changes in writing, sign and date the amendment, and have it witnessed. Attach the amendment to your original living will and make sure all persons who received a copy also receive the amendment.

If the changes you want to make are significant, it is advisable to start from the beginning and re-write your living will. Sign and date the new living will, have it witnessed, and provide a copy to everyone who was given copies of your prior living will.

DURABLE POWER OF ATTORNEY FOR HEALTH CARE

In order to have your wishes concerning medical treatment known and honored should you become incapacitated, you can designate a health care agent by executing what is generally known as a durable power of attorney for health care, also known as a "health care proxy" or "medical power of attorney" in some jurisdictions. In effect, the person you appoint "stands in your shoes" for the purposes of making your health care decisions.

Purpose

Both the living will and the durable power of attorney are types of advance directives, however, they serve two different purposes. The living will, which was developed before the durable power of attorney for health care, sets forth the patient's intentions in case of terminal illness or persistent unconsciousness. A durable power of attorney authorizes a health care agent to make health care decisions for the patient when he or she is no longer capable of making them.

A sample Durable Power of Attorney for Health Care is set forth in the Appendix 17 of this Almanac.

Persons Authorized to Make Health Care Decisions

The individual is always the dominant source for health care decision-making. Even if another person assumes the decision-making role as agent, guardian, or surrogate, the decision-maker must always follow the individual's instructions.

Health Care Agent

As set forth above, an adult or emancipated minor may execute a durable power of attorney for health care and authorize a health care agent to make any health care decisions that he or she could have made while having capacity. Therefore, the appointment of a health care agent must be made very carefully.

In general, a designation of health care agent must be accepted in writing by the person designated to serve in that capacity. Therefore, it is important that you discuss your wishes thoroughly with the person you intend to appoint. You must make sure the person you appoint is comfortable with the directives contained in your living will, and is willing and able to carry out your wishes. The individual must be made aware that they could be called upon to discontinue life-sustaining procedures, and must be willing to take on this responsibility.

Alternate Health Care Agent

It is generally undesirable to appoint a "co-health care agent" as this can lead to disagreements and delays. However, you should designate one or two alternate health care agents. If your first choice for health care agent is not available, or unable to act when health care decisions must be made, the alternate health care agent is called upon to make your health care decisions. Otherwise, health care providers will make treatment decisions for you that follow instructions you gave while you were still able to do so. Any instructions that you write in your living will or durable power of attorney will guide health care providers under these circumstances.

Court-Appointed Guardian

If a guardian has been appointed by the court for the patient, the guardian may not revoke the health care agent's authority unless the court specifically authorizes a revocation. The health care agent's decision under an unrevoked power of attorney takes precedence over the guardian's decision. However, if there is no health care agent appointed, a guardian may make health-care decisions on behalf of the patient.

Surrogate

If the patient has not appointed a health care agent, and there is no court-appointed guardian, a surrogate may assume the authority to make health care decisions for the patient in the same manner as a health care agent under a durable power of attorney. A patient selects a surrogate by advising his or her health care provider of their choice for surrogate.

Relative

If a patient does not select a surrogate to make his or her health care decisions, then an individual related to the patient can step forward and assume the authority. Following is a list of family members, in priority order, who are generally authorized to make health care decisions of a patient if the patient did not select a health care agent or surrogate:

1. Spouse;

2. Adult child;

3. Parent; or

4. Adult brother or sister.

If there is no available relative, the authority to make health care decisions for the patient may be assumed by an adult who has exhibited special care and concern for the patient, who is familiar with the patient's personal values, and who is willing and able to make a health care decision for the patient.

If the health care provider is unable to find any person who can qualify as a surrogate, the health care provider may ask a court to appoint a surrogate to make health care decisions for the patient.

Exclusions

Most states exclude the following people from appointment as a patient's health care agent:

1. The patient's doctor or other treating health care provider;

2. A non-relative employee of the patient's hospital or health care provider;

3. An operator of the patient's nursing home or assisted living facility;

4. A non-relative employee of the patient's nursing home or assisted living facility.

In addition, in some states, the divorce, dissolution, or annulment of the patient's marriage revokes the designation of the patient's former spouse as health care agent. If, following divorce, dissolution or annulment of the patient's marriage, the patient still desires a former spouse to act as their health care agent, they must state their choice in their health care agent designation, or in their order of divorce, dissolution, or annulment of marriage.

Treatment Decisions

The health care agent must make decisions regarding the providing, withholding, or withdrawing of life-sustaining treatment or artificially provided nutrition and hydration according to the patient's specific instructions contained in the patient's living will, if one was executed, or other instructions.

If there are no specific directions concerning a certain course of treatment, the health care agent's decisions must conform as closely as possible to what the patient would have wanted under the circumstances. The health care agent must take into account the patient's personal beliefs, moral values, religious view, etc.

The health care agent exercises a lot of control over your health care and possible outcome if you become incapacitated. Thus, in writing your durable power of attorney, you must consider the scope of your health care agent's authority. You can limit your health care agent's authority, or you can give your health care agent very broad authority.

In general, you can give your health care agent the authority to:

1. Consent to, or refuse, medical treatment and procedures;

2. Employ or dismiss your health care providers;

3. Choose your health care facility;

4. Access your medical records;

5. Consent to pain and comfort medication;

6. Withhold hydration and nutrition; and

7. Take any other steps necessary to carry out your health care instructions.

However, unless your living will specifically provides that nutrition and hydration may be withdrawn or withheld, the health care agent is generally not permitted to make this decision.

Some jurisdictions prohibit a health care agent to consent to certain procedures, including:

1. Voluntary inpatient mental health services;

2. Convulsive treatment (i.e., electro-shock treatment);

3. Pschosurgery (i.e., lobotomies);

4. Abortion; and

5. Neglect of the patient through omission of care primarily intended to provide for the patient's comfort, such as pain-reducing medicine.

DURABLE POWER OF ATTORNEY

The Durable Power of Attorney is an alternative to a guardianship/ conservatorship. The Durable Power of Attorney is a legal document that authorizes someone to make decisions and transact business for the principal in case he or she becomes incapacitated and unable to carry out his or her own affairs. The person who is appointed is called the "agent" or "attorney in fact," however, he or she does not have to be an attorney.

The Durable Power of Attorney is a relatively inexpensive and simple legal method of managing one's financial affairs when he or she becomes incapacitated. An important advantage of the Durable Power of Attorney is that the attorney in fact does not have access to the principal's assets, and, thus, cannot use them for his or her own benefit. In addition, the Durable Power of Attorney terminates upon the principal's death.

Because the Durable Power of Attorney gives the attorney in fact the power to transact business on behalf of the principal, it is important to appoint someone who is trustworthy to act in this capacity. In addition, the attorney in fact should have the knowledge, skill, and ability to carry out the actions authorized in the power of attorney.

Executing the Durable Power of Attorney

In order to have a valid Durable Power of Attorney, the principal must be mentally competent at the time the document is executed. In addition, the Durable Power of Attorney must be acknowledged and executed before a notary public. Once the principal becomes mentally incapacitated, he or she cannot legally appoint someone to act as his or her agent.

file the acceptance of appointment and the appointing instrument with the court of the [county] in which the minor resides or is present; and (2) give written notice of the acceptance of appointment to the appointing parent, if living, the minor, if the minor has attained 14 years of age, and a person other than the parent having care and custody of the minor.

(e) Unless the appointment was previously confirmed by the court, the notice given under subsection (d)(2) must include a statement of the right of those notified to terminate the appointment by filing a written objection in the court as provided in Section 203.

(f) Unless the appointment was previously confirmed by the court, within 30 days after filing the notice and the appointing instrument, a guardian shall petition the court for confirmation of the appointment, giving notice in the manner provided in Section 205(a).

(g) The appointment of a guardian by a parent does not supersede the parental rights of either parent. If both parents are dead or have been adjudged incapacitated persons, an appointment by the last parent who died or was adjudged incapacitated has priority. An appointment by a parent which is effected by filing the guardian's acceptance under a will probated in the State of the testator's domicile is effective in this State.

(h) The powers of a guardian who timely complies with the requirements of subsections (d) and (f) relate back to give acts by the guardian which are of benefit to the minor and occurred on or after the date the appointment became effective the same effect as those that occurred after the filing of the acceptance of the appointment.

(I) The authority of a guardian appointed under this section terminates upon the first to occur of the appointment of a guardian by the court or the giving of written notice to the guardian of the filing of an objection pursuant to Section 203.

Unlike the majority of state statutes, the uniform law does not address the right of concurrent decision-making between the guardian and parent. In addition, under Section 203, a minor who is at least 14 years old and/or the non-custodial parent may attempt to prevent or terminate the appointment by filing a written objection with the court. The objection must be filed prior to the court's confirmation of the appointment. However, the court may still appoint the person chosen by the parent despite the objection.

The principal must explicitly state the authority he or she wants to give the attorney in fact, to avoid the need for appointment of a guardian/conservator. For example, if the power of attorney fails to include an important power, such as the authority to carry on the principal's business during his or her incapacity, a guardianship/conservatorship may be deemed necessary. Alternatively, if the principal wants to limit the attorney in fact's authority in some area, this exclusion should also be explicitly stated in the power of attorney.

The Meaning of "Durable"

A general power of attorney appointment usually ends upon the mental disability of the principal. Therefore, the term "durable" must be included to indicate that the power of attorney appointment does not cease once the principal becomes mentally incapacitated. In fact, in some cases, the durable power of attorney only becomes effective upon the principal's incapacity, e.g., where the principal previously conducted his or her own business transactions without appointing an attorney in fact.

Therefore, depending on the situation, it is important to include explicit language in the power of attorney that the appointment continues—or becomes effective—after the principal becomes incapacitated. Typical clauses read as follows:

1. This power of attorney shall continue to be in effect upon the disability or incapacity of the principal; or

2. This power of attorney becomes effective upon the disability or incapacity of the principal.

Revoking the Durable Power of Attorney

The principal may revoke a Durable Power of Attorney at any time. However, in order to effectively cancel the Durable Power of Attorney, the principal must notify the named attorney in fact as well as any third parties with whom the attorney in fact may have transacted business on the principal's behalf. This may include attorneys, banks, real estate agents, accountants, etc.

Notice should be sent by certified mail, return receipt requested. Revocation is not effective until the third party receives actual notice of the cancellation of the attorney in fact's appointment under the power of attorney. However, if it is urgent that the power of attorney be immediately revoked, third parties should be notified by telephone, and the certified notice should follow. In most cases, third parties will not accept a power of attorney if there is any indication that it may not be effective.

SOCIAL SECURITY REPRESENTATIVE PAYEE

Authority of the Representative Payee

If an individual entitled to receive Social Security or SSI benefits is legally incompetent or otherwise mentally or physically incapable of managing his or her benefits, another individual may be designated by the Social Security Administration (SSA) to act on the incapacitated person's behalf. The designated individual is known as a "representative payee."

The Representative Payee is authorized to receive the monthly Social Security or SSI income of the person entitled to the money—i.e., the beneficiary—which is to be used for the benefit of the beneficiary. A social security recipient can avoid guardianship/conservatorship by appointing someone they trust to be their Representative Payee in case they are unable to handle their own money.

Necessity of the Representative Payee

It is not necessary that the beneficiary be deemed legally incapacitated to appoint a Representative Payee. The beneficiary simply must need assistance in handling their Social Security income. The Social Security Administration (SSA) will consider the following information to determine whether a Representative Payee is necessary:

1. A certified copy of a court determination of legal incapacity dated within the past year;

2. Medical evidence such as a statement by a physician, based on a recent examination of the beneficiary and knowledge of the beneficiary's present condition, provided it includes an opinion as to whether the beneficiary is able to manage his or her benefit payments; or

3. A statement by the beneficiary, the beneficiary's relatives, and other persons who are in a position to know and observe the beneficiary.

Appointment of the Representative Payee

The beneficiary may appoint another person or an organization to be their Representative Payee, however, the SSA will conduct an investigation before the Representative Payee may be appointed. The SSA is supposed to make sure the individual or organization will best serve the interests of the beneficiary. For example, although a friend or custodial institution—e.g., a nursing home—can be designated as a representative payee, the SSA prefers to appoint relatives who are personally concerned for the beneficiary.

Thus, in approving a Representative Payee, the SSA considers:

1. The relationship between the proposed Representative Payee and the beneficiary;

2. Whether the proposed Representative Payee has any legal authority over the beneficiary; and

3. Whether the proposed Representative Payee is in a position to know of and look after the needs of the beneficiary.

In addition, the SSA uses "flexible preferences" to determine who would be an appropriate Representative Payee for the beneficiary, in the following order:

1. A legal guardian, spouse, or other relative, who has custody of the beneficiary or who demonstrates strong concern for the personal welfare of the beneficiary;

2. A friend who has custody of the beneficiary or who demonstrates strong concern for the personal welfare of the beneficiary;

3. A public or non-profit agency having custody of the beneficiary;

4. A private institution operated for profit and licensed under state law, which has custody of the beneficiary; and

5. Persons other than the above who are qualified to carry out the responsibilities of a payee and who are able and willing to serve as a payee for the beneficiary.

A beneficiary has the right to appeal a decision by the SSA, e.g., regarding appointment of a Representative Payee—to an Administrative Law Judge. However, an individual who is denied appointment as a Representative Payee does not have a right to appeal the SSA decision.

The SSA Request to be Selected as Representative Payee (Form SSA-11-BK) is set forth at Appendix 18 of this Almanac.

Duties of the Representative Payee

The Social Security or SSI benefits are sent directly to the Representative Payee who must manage the funds for the personal care and well-being of the beneficiary, and pay the beneficiary's bills from the funds. The Representative Payee is required to use the social security payments only for the use and benefit of the beneficiary, and in the best interest of the beneficiary.

Any remaining funds do not belong to the Representative Payee, but must be saved for the benefit of the recipient. The SSA requires the

Representative Payee to file yearly accounting reports that set forth the manner in which the social security benefits were used on behalf of the beneficiary.

In addition, the Representative Payee must notify the SSA of any event that will affect the amount of benefits or the beneficiary's right to benefits. The Representative Payee must also notify the SSA of any changes in circumstances that may affect his or her performance of their responsibilities as Representative Payee.

Use of the Benefits

The Representative Payee must use the social security income only for the use and benefit of the beneficiary, as follows:

Current Maintenance of the Beneficiary

Current maintenance of the beneficiary includes the cost of shelter, clothing, medical care, and personal comfort items. If the beneficiary is institutionalized due to mental or physical incapacity, the customary cost of institutional care is permissible. In addition, payment for items that will assist the beneficiary's recovery or release from the institution, or payment for personal items that will improve the beneficiary's condition while institutionalized, are also authorized.

Support of the Beneficiary's Family

If the beneficiary's current maintenance needs are met, the Representative Payee may use part of the benefits to support the beneficiary's legally dependent spouse, child, and/or parent.

Debts of the Beneficiary

If the beneficiary's current and reasonably foreseeable needs are met, the Representative Payee may pay debts of the beneficiary that arose before he or she was appointed, although the Representative Payee is not required to pay such prior debts.

Accounting Requirement

Under federal law, the Representative Payee is required to provide an annual accounting of the social security benefits he or she receives on behalf of the beneficiary. In addition, the SSA may require periodic written reports, and may verify how the Representative Payee used the funds. Therefore, it is important that the Representative Payee keep detailed records of how the benefits were used.

Replacement of the Representative Payee

The SSA has the authority to remove a Representative Payee and appoint a replacement. This may occur under the following circumstances:

1. The death of the Representative Payee;

2. The failure of the Representative Payee to provide information, accounting or other evidence requested by the SSA;

3. The improper use of the benefit payments by the Representative Payee;

4. The inability of the Representative Payee to manage the benefit payments;

5. The Representative Payee's request to no longer act as a Representative Payee; or

6. Failure of the Representative Payee to carry out any of his or her other required responsibilities.

Restoring the Beneficiary as Payee

If the beneficiary is able to demonstrate the mental and physical ability to manage, or direct the management of the social security benefits, he or she will be restored as the payee and will again receive direct payment of the social security benefits. The SSA will consider the following information to determine whether the beneficiary should be restored as payee:

1. A certified copy of a court order restoring the beneficiary's rights if he or she had previously been adjudged legally incapacitated;

2. A medical statement showing the beneficiary's ability to manage or direct the management of his or her benefit payments; or

3. Other evidence establishing the beneficiary's ability to manage, or direct the management of, his or her benefit payments.

TRUSTS

A trust is a legal device that permits one person (the "trustee") to manage property and money for the benefit of another person (the "beneficiary") in accordance with the directions of the person who set up the trust (the "settlor"). A living trust is created while the settlor is still alive. The success of a trust depends on the selection of the trustee, i.e., the person or agency that will administer the trust.

Revocable Living Trust

A Revocable Living Trust is particularly useful in the event the settlor becomes incapacitated. The settlor can also serve as the trustee and beneficiary of the trust so he or she can maintain control over the trust. Although the settlor must be competent when he or she sets up the trust, an alternate trustee can be named to manage the trust in case the settlor becomes incapacitated.

If parents are concerned about how a disabled individual will manage an inheritance, a trust fund may be established instead of a guardianship.

In the event of the settlor's death, the trust document generally provides for distribution of the settlor's assets without the necessity of a will. The assets can be distributed directly to the beneficiaries without court intervention.

JOINT TENANCY ACCOUNTS

A joint tenancy permits one person to authorize another person (the "joint tenant") to access their funds if he or she becomes incapacitated. However, one must be very careful in choosing their joint tenant because once authorized, he or she can withdraw all of the funds in the joint account.

In community property jurisdictions, one spouse is permitted to manage the community property of the incapacitated spouse.

SKILLS TRAINING

Many disabled people are able to manage their own personal or financial affairs without the intervention of a guardian/conservator provided they receive appropriate services and support. For example, handicapped persons who receive skills training are usually capable of independent living.

If there is a deficit in a particular area, such as financial management, there are agencies that provide assistance with tasks such as budgeting and paying bills, if there are no family members who are able to assist with such activities.

In addition, most states provide protective services for persons needing assistance in managing their resources, carrying out the activities of daily living, or protecting themselves from neglect or hazardous or abusive situations.

ADVANCE DESIGNATION OF GUARDIAN

If it turns out that one or more of the alternatives to guardianship/conservatorship described herein cannot be carried out—e.g., because the designated health care agent or attorney in fact are unable to take on the responsibility—the appointment of a guardian/conservator may be required for a person who becomes incapacitated. To prepare for this possibility in advance, an individual may designate a person to act as his or her guardian in case he or she subsequently becomes incapacitated.

The individual must be a mentally competent adult at the time he or she designates a guardian in advance. Generally, a sworn declaration, properly signed by the declarant before two witnesses, will suffice as evidence of the designation of guardian. Neither of the witnesses can be named as the guardian in the declaration. In addition, if the designated guardian is the spouse, a later divorce will disqualify the spouse as the designated guardian.

If the declarant becomes incapacitated, the sworn declaration may be filed with the appropriate court, along with the application for appointment of a guardian. In general, the court will appoint the designated guardian unless it determines that the designated guardian would not serve the best interests of the incapacitated person, or is otherwise disqualified to serve as guardian.

The designation of guardian may be revoked by the declarant while he or she is still mentally competent by:

(1) execution of a new declaration; or

(2) cancellation of the declaration, e.g., by destroying it.

APPENDIX 1:
GUARDIANSHIP AUTHORIZATION AFFIDAVIT

Guardianship Authorization

MINOR
Name: _____
Birthdate: _____ Age: _____ Year in School _____

MOTHER
Name: _____
Street Address: _____
City: _____ State: _____ Zip Code: _____
Home Phone: _____ Work phone: _____

FATHER
Name: _____
Street Address: _____
City: _____ State: _____ Zip Code: _____
Home Phone: _____ Work phone: _____

PROPOSED GUARDIAN(S)
Name: _____
Street Address: _____
City: _____ State: _____ Zip Code: _____
Home Phone: _____ Work phone: _____
Relationship to minor: _____

Name: _____
Street Address: _____
City: _____ State: _____ Zip Code: _____
Home Phone: _____ Work phone: _____
Relationship to minor: _____

In case of emergency, if proposed guardian cannot be reached, please contact:_____ Phone: _____

Authorization And Consent Of Parent(s)

1.   I affirm that the minor indicated above is my child and that I have legal custody of her/him. I give my full authorization and consent for my child to live with the proposed guardian(s), or for the proposed guardian to set a place of residence for my child.

2.   I give the proposed guardian permission to act in my place and to make decisions pertaining to my child's educational and religious activities, including, but not limited to enrollment, permission to participate in activities and consent for medical treatment at school.

1 of 3

GUARDIANSHIP AUTHORIZATION

3. I give the proposed guardian permission to authorize medical and dental care for my child, including, but not limited to, medical examinations, X-rays, tests, anesthetic, surgical operations, hospital care or other treatments that, in the proposed guardian's sole opinion, are needed or useful for my child. Such medical treatment shall only be provided upon the advice of, and supervision by, a physician, surgeon or dentist or other medical practitioner licensed to practice in the United States.

4. I give the proposed guardian permission to apply for benefits on my child's behalf, including, but not limited to, Social Security, public assistance, health insurance, and Veterans' Administration benefits.

5. I give the proposed guardian permission to apply and obtain for my child any or all of the following: Social Security number, Social Security card, and U.S. passport.

6. This authorization shall cover the period from _____ to _____ .

7. During the period when the proposed guardian cares for my child, the costs of my child's upkeep, living expenses, medical and dental expenses shall be paid as follows:

_____

_____

_____

I declare under penalty of perjury under the laws of the State of California that the foregoing is true and correct.

Mother's signature: _____ Date: _____

Father's signature: _____ Date: _____

Consent Of Proposed Guardian

I solemnly affirm that I will assume full responsibility for the minor who will live with me during the period designated above. I agree to make necessary decisions and to provide consent for the minor as set forth I the above Authorization & Consent by Parent(s). I also agree to the terms of the costs of the minor's up keep, living expenses, medical and/or dental expenses set forth in the above Authorization and Consent of Parent(s).

I declare under penalty of perjury under the laws of the State of California that the foregoing is true and correct.

Proposed Guardian's Signature: _____ Date: _____

2 of 3

GUARDIANSHIP AUTHORIZATION

CERTIFICATE OF ACKNOWLEDGMENT OF NOTARY PUBLIC

STATE OF CALIFORNIA   )
) ss.
COUNTY OF SANTA CLARA   )

On _____, before me, the undersigned, a Notary Public, in and for said county and state, duly commissioned and sworn, personally appeared _____, personally known to me or proved to me on the basis of satisfactory evidence to be the person whose name is subscribed to the within instrument, and acknowledged to me that s/he executed the same in her/his authorized capacity, and that by her/his signature on the instrument the person, or the entity upon behalf of which the person acted, executed the instrument.

WITNESS MY HAND AND OFFICIAL SEAL.

_____

STATE OF CALIFORNIA   )
) ss.
COUNTY OF SANTA CLARA   )

On _____, before me, the undersigned, a Notary Public, in and for said county and state, duly commissioned and sworn, personally appeared _____, personally known to me or proved to me on the basis of satisfactory evidence to be the person whose name is subscribed to the within instrument, and acknowledged to me that s/he executed the same in her/his authorized capacity, and that by her/his signature on the instrument the person, or the entity upon behalf of which the person acted, executed the instrument.

WITNESS MY HAND AND OFFICIAL SEAL.

_____

STATE OF CALIFORNIA   )
) ss.
COUNTY OF SANTA CLARA   )

On _____, before me, the undersigned, a Notary Public, in and for said county and state, duly commissioned and sworn, personally appeared _____, personally known to me or proved to me on the basis of satisfactory evidence to be the person whose name is subscribed to the within instrument, and acknowledged to me that s/he executed the same in her/his authorized capacity, and that by her/his signature on the instrument the person, or the entity upon behalf of which the person acted, executed the instrument.

WITNESS MY HAND AND OFFICIAL SEAL.

_____

GUARDIANSHIP AUTHORIZATION

APPENDIX 2:
PETITION FOR GUARDIANSHIP
OF A MINOR

ATTORNEY OR PARTY WITHOUT ATTORNEY *(Name, State Bar number, and address):*	FOR COURT USE ONLY
TELEPHONE NO.: FAX NO. *(Optional):* E-MAIL ADDRESS *(Optional):* ATTORNEY FOR *(Name):*	

SUPERIOR COURT OF CALIFORNIA, COUNTY OF
STREET ADDRESS:
MAILING ADDRESS:
CITY AND ZIP CODE:
BRANCH NAME:

GUARDIANSHIP OF *(Name):*	CASE NUMBER:
MINOR	

PETITION FOR APPOINTMENT OF GUARDIAN OF ☐ **MINOR** ☐ **MINORS** ☐ Person* ☐ Estate*	HEARING DATE AND TIME:	DEPT.:

1. **Petitioner** *(name each):*

   requests that

   a. ☐ *(Name):*
   (Address and telephone):

   be appointed guardian of the PERSON of the minor or minors named in item 2 and Letters issue upon qualification.

   b. ☐ *(Name):*
   (Address and telephone):

   be appointed guardian of the ESTATE of the minor or minors named in item 2 and Letters issue upon qualification.

   c. (1) ☐ bond not be required ☐ because the petition is for guardian of the person only ☐ because the proposed guardian is a corporate fiduciary or an exempt government agency ☐ for the reasons stated in Attachment 1c.

      (2) ☐ $ bond be fixed. It will be furnished by an authorized surety company or as otherwise provided by law.
      (Specify reasons in Attachment 1c if the amount is different from the minimum required by Prob. Code, § 8482.)

      (3) ☐ $ in deposits in a blocked account be allowed. Receipts will be filed.
      (Specify institution and location):

d. ☐ authorization be granted under Probate Code section 2590 to exercise the powers specified in Attachment 9.

e. ☐ orders relating to the powers and duties of the proposed guardian of the person under Probate Code sections 2351–2358 be granted *(specify orders, facts, and reasons in Attachment 1e).*

f. ☐ an order dispensing with notice to the persons named in Attachment 10 be granted.

g. ☐ other orders be granted *(specify in Attachment 1g).*

2. Attached is a copy of *Guardianship Petition—Child Information Attachment* (form GC-210(CA)) for **each** minor for whom this petition requests the appointment of a guardian. The full legal name and date of birth of each minor is :

   a. Name: Date of Birth *(month/day/year):*

   b. Name: Date of Birth *(month/day/year):*

   c. Name: Date of Birth *(month/day/year):*

   d. Name: Date of Birth *(month/day/year):*

   ☐ The names and dates of birth of additional minors are specified on Attachment 2 to this petition.

* **You MAY use this form or form GC-210(P) for a guardianship of the person. You MUST use this form for a guardianship of the estate or the person and estate. Do NOT use this form for a temporary guardianship.**   Page 1 of 3

Form Adopted for Mandatory
and Alternative Mandatory Use
Instead of Form GC-210(P)
Judicial Council of California
GC-210 [Rev. January 1, 2007]

PETITION FOR APPOINTMENT OF GUARDIAN OF MINOR
(Probate—Guardianships and Conservatorships)

Probate Code, § 1510;
Cal. Rules of Court, rule 7.101
www.courtinfo.ca.gov

GC-210

GUARDIANSHIP OF *(Name)*:	CASE NUMBER:
MINOR	

3. Petitioner is

    a. ☐ related to the minor or minors named in item 2, as shown in item 7 of each minor's attached form GC-210(CA).

    b. ☐ the minor named in item 2, who is 12 years of age or older.

    c. ☐ other person on behalf of minor or minors named in item 2, as shown in item 7 of each minor's attached form
       GC-210(CA).

4. The proposed guardian is *(check all that apply)*:

    a. ☐ a nominee *(affix a copy of nomination as Attachment 4 or file* Nomination of Guardian *(form GC-211, items 2 and 3)* with
       this petition.

    b. ☐ related to the minor or minors named in item 2, as shown in item 3 of each minor's attached form GC-210(CA).

    c. ☐ other, as shown in item 3 of each minor's attached form GC-210(CA).

5. ☐ Petitioner, with intent to adopt, has accepted or intends to accept physical care or custody of the minor.

6. ☐ A person other than the proposed guardian has been nominated as the guardian of the minor by ☐ will ☐ other
    writing. A copy of the nomination is affixed as Attachment 6. *(Specify name and address of nominee in item 2 of minor's
    attached form GC-210(CA).)*

7. ☐ **Character and estimated value of property of the estate** *(complete if petition requests appointment of a guardian of
    the estate or the person and estate):*

    a. Personal property: $

    b. Annual gross income from all sources, including real
       and personal property, wages, pensions, and public benefits: $ _____

    c. **Total:** $ _____

    d. Real property: $

8. Appointment of a guardian of the ☐ person ☐ estate of the minor or minors named in item 2 is necessary or
    convenient for the following reasons:

    ☐ Continued in Attachment 8.   ☐ Parental custody would be detrimental to the minor or minors named in item 2.

9. ☐ Granting the proposed guardian of the estate powers to be exercised independently under Probate Code section 2590
    would be to the advantage and benefit and in the best interest of the guardianship estate. Reasons for this request and
    the powers requested are specified in Attachment 9.

10. ☐ Notice to the persons named in Attachment 10 should be dispensed with under Probate Code section 1511 because

    ☐ they cannot with reasonable diligence be given notice *(specify names and efforts to locate in Attachment 10).*

    ☐ giving notice to them would be contrary to the interest of justice *(specify names and reasons in Attachment 10).*

GC-210 [Rev. January 1, 2007]   **PETITION FOR APPOINTMENT OF GUARDIAN OF MINOR**   Page 2 of 3
                     (Probate—Guardianships and Conservatorships)

GC-210

GUARDIANSHIP OF (Name):	CASE NUMBER:
MINOR	

11. ☐ (Complete this item if this petition is filed by a person who is not related to a minor named in item 2 and is not a petition for appointment of a guardian of the estate only.)

   a. ☐   Petitioner is the proposed guardian and will promptly furnish all information requested by any agency referred to in Probate Code section 1543.

   b. ☐   Petitioner is not the proposed guardian. A statement by the proposed guardian that he or she will promptly furnish all information requested by any agency referred to in Probate Code section 1543 is affixed as Attachment 11b.

   c. The proposed guardian's home ☐ is ☐ is not a licensed foster family home.

   d. ☐   The proposed guardian has never filed a petition for adoption of the minor ☐ except as specified in Attachment 11d.

12. ☐   Attached to this petition is a *Declaration Under Uniform Child Custody Jurisdiction and Enforcement Act (UCCJEA)* (form FL-105/GC-120) concerning all children listed in item 2. *(Guardianship of the person or the person and estate.)*

13. Filed with this petition are the following *(check all that apply)*:

   ☐ *Consent of Proposed Guardian* (form GC-211, item 1)
   ☐ *Nomination of Guardian* (form GC-211, items 2 and 3)
   ☐ *Consent to Appointment of Guardian and Waiver* of Notice (form GC-211, item 4)
   ☐ *Petition for Appointment of Temporary Guardian* (form GC-110)
   ☐ *Petition for Appointment of Temporary Guardian of the Person* (form GC-110(P))
   ☐ *Confidential Guardianship Screening Form* (form GC-212)
   ☐ Other *(specify):*

14. All attachments to this form are incorporated by this reference as though placed here in this form. There are _____ pages attached to this form.

Date: _____

▶ _____
(SIGNATURE OF ATTORNEY*)

* **(All petitioners must also sign (Prob. Code, § 1020).)**

I declare under penalty of perjury under the laws of the State of California that the foregoing is true and correct.

Date: _____

_____
(TYPE OR PRINT NAME)

▶ _____
(SIGNATURE OF PETITIONER)

_____
(TYPE OR PRINT NAME)

▶ _____
(SIGNATURE OF PETITIONER)

_____
(TYPE OR PRINT NAME)

▶ _____
(SIGNATURE OF PETITIONER)

GC-210 [Rev. January 1, 2007]

PETITION FOR APPOINTMENT OF GUARDIAN OF MINOR
(Probate—Guardianships and Conservatorships)

Page 3 of 3

APPENDIX 3:
NOTICE OF GUARDIANSHIP HEARING

GC-020

ATTORNEY OR PARTY WITHOUT ATTORNEY *(Name, State Bar number, and address)*:	FOR COURT USE ONLY
TELEPHONE NO.: FAX NO. *(Optional)*: E-MAIL ADDRESS *(Optional)*: ATTORNEY FOR *(Name)*:	

SUPERIOR COURT OF CALIFORNIA, COUNTY OF

    STREET ADDRESS:

    MAILING ADDRESS:

    CITY AND ZIP CODE:

    BRANCH NAME:

☐ GUARDIANSHIP ☐ CONSERVATORSHIP OF THE ☐ PERSON ☐ ESTATE

OF *(Name)*:

☐ MINOR ☐ (PROPOSED) CONSERVATEE

NOTICE OF HEARING—GUARDIANSHIP OR CONSERVATORSHIP	CASE NUMBER:

This notice is required by law.
This notice does not require you to appear in court, but you may attend the hearing if you wish.

1. NOTICE is given that *(name)*:
   (representative capacity, if any):
   has filed *(specify)*:

2. You may refer to documents on file in this proceeding for more information. *(Some documents filed with the court are confidential. Under some circumstances you or your attorney may be able to see or receive copies of confidential documents if you file papers in the proceeding or apply to the court.)*

3. ☐ The petition includes an application for the independent exercise of powers by a guardian or conservator under
   ☐ Probate Code section 2108 ☐ Probate Code section 2590.
   Powers requested are ☐ specified below ☐ specified in Attachment 3.

APPENDIX 4:
LETTERS OF GUARDIANSHIP

ATTORNEY OR PARTY WITHOUT ATTORNEY *(Name, state bar number, and address)*:	TELEPHONE AND FAX NOS.:	*FOR COURT USE ONLY*
ATTORNEY FOR *(Name)*:		

SUPERIOR COURT OF CALIFORNIA, COUNTY OF

STREET ADDRESS:
MAILING ADDRESS:
CITY AND ZIP CODE:
BRANCH NAME:

GUARDIANSHIP OF *(Name)*:

MINOR

LETTERS OF GUARDIANSHIP ☐ Person ☐ Estate	CASE NUMBER:

LETTERS

1. *(Name)*:
   is appointed guardian of the ☐ person ☐ estate
   of *(name)*:
2. ☐ Other powers have been granted and conditions have
   been imposed as follows:
   a. ☐ Powers to be exercised independently under
   Probate Code section 2590 as specified in
   Attachment 2a *(specify powers, restrictions,
   conditions, and limitations)*.
   b. ☐ Conditions relating to the care and custody of
   the property under Probate Code section
   2402 as specified in Attachment 2b.
   c. ☐ Conditions relating to the care, treatment,
   education, and welfare of the minor under
   Probate Code section 2358 as specified in
   Attachment 2c.
   d. ☐ Other *(specify in Attachment 2d)*.
3. ☐ The guardian is not authorized to take possession of
   money or any other property without a specific court
   order.

4. Number of pages attached: _____

WITNESS, clerk of the court, with seal of the court affixed.

(SEAL)	Date:
	Clerk, by
	_____
	(DEPUTY)

AFFIRMATION

I solemnly affirm that I will perform the duties of guardian
according to law.

Executed on *(date)*:

at *(place)*:

▶ _____
(SIGNATURE OF APPOINTEE)

CERTIFICATION

I certify that this document and any attachments is a correct
copy of the original on file in my office, and that the *Letters*
issued to the person appointed above have not been revoked,
annulled, or set aside and are still in full force and effect.

WITNESS, clerk of the court, with seal of the court affixed.

(SEAL)	Date:
	Clerk, by
	_____
	(DEPUTY)

Form Approved by the
Judicial Council of California
GC-250 [Rev. January 1, 1998]

LETTERS OF GUARDIANSHIP

Probate Code, §§ 2310,
2311

APPENDIX 5:
ORDER APPOINTING GUARDIAN
OF MINOR

GC-240

ATTORNEY OR PARTY WITHOUT ATTORNEY *(Name, state bar number, and address)*:	TELEPHONE AND FAX NOS.:	*FOR COURT USE ONLY*

ATTORNEY FOR *(Name)*:

SUPERIOR COURT OF CALIFORNIA, COUNTY OF
STREET ADDRESS:
MAILING ADDRESS:
CITY AND ZIP CODE:
BRANCH NAME:

GUARDIANSHIP OF THE ☐ PERSON ☐ ESTATE OF *(Name)*:

MINOR

ORDER APPOINTING GUARDIAN OF ☐ **MINOR** ☐ **MINORS**	CASE NUMBER:

WARNING: THIS APPOINTMENT IS NOT EFFECTIVE UNTIL LETTERS HAVE ISSUED.

1. The petition for appointment of guardian came on for hearing as follows *(check boxes c, d, and e to indicate personal presence)*:

   a. Judge *(name)*:
   b. Hearing date: Time: ☐ Dept.:   ☐ Room:

   c. ☐ Petitioner *(name)*:
   d. ☐ Attorney for Petitioner *(name)*:
   e. ☐ Attorney for minor *(name, address, and telephone)*:

THE COURT FINDS

2. a. ☐ All notices required by law have been given.
   b. ☐ Notice of hearing to the following persons ☐ has been ☐ should be dispensed with *(names)*:

3. ☐ Appointment of a guardian of the ☐ person ☐ estate of the minor is necessary and convenient.

4. ☐ Granting the guardian powers to be exercised independently under Probate Code section 2590 is to the advantage and benefit and is in the best interest of the guardianship estate.

5. ☐ Attorney *(name)*: has been appointed by the court as legal counsel to represent the minor in these proceedings. The cost for representation is: $

6. ☐ The appointed court investigator, probation officer, or domestic relations investigator is *(name, title, address, and telephone)*:

THE COURT ORDERS
7. a. *(Name)*:
   (Address):   *(Telephone)*:

   is appointed guardian of the PERSON of *(name)*:
   and *Letters* shall issue upon qualification.

Do NOT use this form for a temporary guardianship.   (Continued on reverse)

Form Approved by the
Judicial Council of California   **ORDER APPOINTING GUARDIAN OF MINOR**   Probate Code, §§ 1514,
GC-240 [Rev. January 1, 1998]   2310

GUARDIANSHIP OF *(Name)*:	CASE NUMBER:
MINOR	

7. b. *(Name)*:
   (Address):   *(Telephone)*:

   is appointed guardian of the ESTATE of *(name)*:
   and *Letters* shall issue upon qualification.

8. ☐ Notice of hearing to the persons named in item 2b is dispensed with.

9. a. ☐ Bond is not required.
   b. ☐ Bond is fixed at: $ to be furnished by an authorized surety company or as otherwise
      provided by law.
   c. ☐ Deposits of: $ are ordered to be placed in a blocked account at *(specify institution and
      location)*:

      and receipts shall be filed. No withdrawals shall be made without a court order. ☐ Additional orders in Attachment 9c.
   d. ☐ The guardian is not authorized to take possession of money or any other property without a specific court order.

10. ☐ For legal services rendered on behalf of the minor,   ☐ parents of the minor   ☐ minor's estate   shall pay to
    (name):   the sum of: $
    ☐ forthwith   ☐ as follows *(specify terms, including any combination of payors)*:

11. ☐ The guardian of the estate is granted authorization under Probate Code section 2590 to exercise independently the powers
    specified in Attachment 11   ☐ subject to the conditions provided.

12. ☐ Orders are granted relating to the powers and duties of the guardian of the person under Probate Code sections 2351-2358
    as specified in Attachment 12.

13. ☐ Orders are granted relating to the conditions imposed under Probate Code section 2402 upon the guardian of the estate as
    specified in Attachment 13.

14. ☐ Other orders as specified in Attachment 14 are granted.

15. ☐ The probate referee appointed is *(name and address)*:

16. Number of boxes checked in items 8-15: _____

17. Number of pages attached: _____

Date:

_____
JUDGE OF THE SUPERIOR COURT
☐ SIGNATURE FOLLOWS LAST ATTACHMENT

GC-240 [Rev. January, 1 1998]   **ORDER APPOINTING GUARDIAN OF MINOR**   Page two

APPENDIX 6:
CAPACITY DECLARATION

TELEPHONE NO.: FAX NO. *(Optional)*: E-MAIL ADDRESS *(Optional)*: ATTORNEY FOR *(Name)*:	

SUPERIOR COURT OF CALIFORNIA, COUNTY OF

STREET ADDRESS:
MAILING ADDRESS:
CITY AND ZIP CODE:
BRANCH NAME:

CONSERVATORSHIP OF THE ☐ PERSON ☐ ESTATE   OF *(Name)*:

☐ CONSERVATEE ☐ PROPOSED CONSERVATEE

CAPACITY DECLARATION—CONSERVATORSHIP	CASE NUMBER

TO PHYSICIAN, PSYCHOLOGIST, OR RELIGIOUS HEALING PRACTITIONER

The purpose of this form is to enable the court to determine whether the (proposed) conservatee *(check all that apply)*:

A. ☐ is able to attend a court hearing to determine whether a conservator should be appointed to care for him or her. The court
hearing is set for *(date)*: [_____] . *(Complete item 5, sign, and file page 1 of this form.)*

B. ☐ has the capacity to give informed consent to medical treatment. *(Complete items 6 through 8, sign page 3, and file pages 1
through 3 of this form.)*

C. ☐ has dementia and, if so, (1) whether he or she needs to be placed in a secured-perimeter residential care facility for the
elderly, and (2) whether he or she needs or would benefit from dementia medications. *(Complete items 6 and 8 of this form
and form GC-335A; sign and attach form GC-335A. File pages 1 through 3 of this form and form GC-335A.)*

*(If more than one item is checked above, sign the last applicable page of this form or form GC-335A if item C is checked. File page 1
through the last applicable page of this form; also file form GC-335A if item C is checked.)*

COMPLETE ITEMS 1–4 OF THIS FORM IN ALL CASES.

GENERAL INFORMATION

1. *(Name)*:

2. *(Office address and telephone number)*:

3. I am
   a. ☐ a California licensed ☐ physician ☐ psychologist acting within the scope of my licensure
      ☐ with at least two years' experience in diagnosing dementia.
   b. ☐ an accredited practitioner of a religion whose tenets and practices call for reliance on prayer alone for healing, which
      religion is adhered to by the (proposed) conservatee. The (proposed) conservatee is under my treatment. *(Religious
      practitioner may make the determination under item 5 ONLY.)*

4. (Proposed) conservatee *(name)*:
   a. I last saw the (proposed) conservatee on *(date)*:
   b. The (proposed) conservatee ☐ is ☐ is NOT a patient under my continuing treatment.

ABILITY TO ATTEND COURT HEARING

5. A court hearing on the petition for appointment of a conservator is set for the date indicated in item A above. *(Complete a or b.)*

    a. ☐   The proposed conservatee is able to attend the court hearing.

    b. ☐   Because of medical inability, the proposed conservatee is NOT able to attend the court hearing *(check all items below that apply)*

        (1) ☐   on the date set *(see date in box in item A above)*.

        (2) ☐   for the foreseeable future.

        (3) ☐   until *(date):*

        (4) **Supporting facts** *(State facts in the space below or check this box* ☐ *and state the facts in Attachment 5):*

I declare under penalty of perjury under the laws of the State of California that the foregoing is true and correct.

Date:

▶

_____
(TYPE OR PRINT NAME)

_____
(SIGNATURE OF DECLARANT)

Page 1 of ___

Form Adopted for Mandatory Use
Judicial Council of California
GC-335 [Rev. January 1, 2004]

CAPACITY DECLARATION—CONSERVATORSHIP

Probate Code, §§ 811,
813, 1801, 1825,
1881, 1910, 2356.5

CONSERVATORSHIP OF THE ☐ PERSON ☐	ESTATE OF *(Name)*:	CASE NUMBER:
☐ CONSERVATEE ☐ PROPOSED CONSERVATEE		

6. **EVALUATION OF (PROPOSED) CONSERVATEE'S MENTAL FUNCTIONS**

Note to practitioner: This form is *not* a rating scale. It is intended to assist you in recording your *impressions* of the (proposed) conservatee's mental abilities. Where appropriate, you may refer to scores on standardized rating instruments.

(Instructions for items 6A–6C): Check the appropriate designation as follows: **a** = no apparent impairment; **b** = moderate impairment; **c** = major impairment; **d** = so impaired as to be incapable of being assessed; **e** = I have no opinion.)

A. **Alertness and attention**

  (1) Levels of arousal (lethargic, responds only to vigorous and persistent stimulation, stupor)
    a ☐   b ☐   c ☐   d ☐   e ☐

  (2) Orientation (types of orientation impaired)
    a ☐   b ☐   c ☐   d ☐   e ☐   Person
    a ☐   b ☐   c ☐   d ☐   e ☐   Time (day, date, month, season, year)
    a ☐   b ☐   c ☐   d ☐   e ☐   Place (address, town, state)
    a ☐   b ☐   c ☐   d ☐   e ☐   Situation ("Why am I here?")

  (3) Ability to attend and concentrate (give detailed answers from memory, mental ability required to thread a needle)
    a ☐   b ☐   c ☐   d ☐   e ☐

B. **Information processing.** Ability to:

  (1) Remember (ability to remember a question before answering; to recall names, relatives, past presidents, and events of the past 24 hours)
    i.   Short-term memory   a ☐   b ☐   c ☐   d ☐   e ☐
    ii   Long-term memory   a ☐   b ☐   c ☐   d ☐   e ☐
    iii   Immediate recall   a ☐   b ☐   c ☐   d ☐   e ☐

  (2) Understand and communicate either verbally or otherwise (deficits reflected by inability to comprehend questions, follow instructions, use words correctly, or name objects; use of nonsense words)
    a ☐   b ☐   c ☐   d ☐   e ☐

  (3) Recognize familiar objects and persons (deficits reflected by inability to recognize familiar faces, objects, etc.)
    a ☐   b ☐   c ☐   d ☐   e ☐

  (4) Understand and appreciate quantities (deficits reflected by inability to perform simple calculations)
    a ☐   b ☐   c ☐   d ☐   e ☐

  (5) Reason using abstract concepts. (deficits reflected by inability to grasp abstract aspects of his or her situation or to interpret idiomatic expressions or proverbs)
    a ☐   b ☐   c ☐   d ☐   e ☐

  (6) Plan, organize, and carry out actions (assuming physical ability) in one's own rational self-interest (deficits reflected by inability to break complex tasks down into simple steps and carry them out)
    a ☐   b ☐   c ☐   d ☐   e ☐

  (7) Reason logically.
    a ☐   b ☐   c ☐   d ☐   e ☐

C. **Thought disorders**

  (1) Severely disorganized thinking (rambling thoughts; nonsensical, incoherent, or nonlinear thinking)
    a ☐   b ☐   c ☐   d ☐   e ☐

  (2) Hallucinations (auditory, visual, olfactory)
    a ☐   b ☐   c ☐   d ☐   e ☐

  (3) Delusions (demonstrably false belief maintained without or against reason or evidence)
    a ☐   b ☐   c ☐   d ☐   e ☐

  (4) Uncontrollable or intrusive thoughts (unwanted compulsive thoughts, compulsive behavior).
    a ☐   b ☐   c ☐   d ☐   e ☐

(Continued on next page)

GC-335 [Rev. January 1, 2004]   **CAPACITY DECLARATION—CONSERVATORSHIP**   Page 2 of 3

CAPACITY DECLARATION

CONSERVATORSHIP OF THE ☐ PERSON ☐ ESTATE OF *(Name)*:	CASE NUMBER:
☐ CONSERVATEE ☐ PROPOSED CONSERVATEE	

6. *(continued)*

D. **Ability to modulate mood and affect.** The (proposed) conservatee ☐ has ☐ does NOT have a pervasive and persistent or recurrent emotional state that appears inappropriate in degree to his or her circumstances. *(If so, complete remainder of item 6D.)* ☐ I have no opinion.

*(**Instructions for item 6D:** Check the degree of impairment of each inappropriate mood state (if any) as follows: **a** = mildly inappropriate; **b** = moderately inappropriate; **c** = severely inappropriate.)*

Anger a ☐ b ☐ c ☐	Euphoria a ☐ b ☐ c ☐	Helplessness a ☐ b ☐ c ☐
Anxiety a ☐ b ☐ c ☐	Depression a ☐ b ☐ c ☐	Apathy a ☐ b ☐ c ☐
Fear a ☐ b ☐ c ☐	Hopelessness a ☐ b ☐ c ☐	Indifference a ☐ b ☐ c ☐
Panic a ☐ b ☐ c ☐	Despair a ☐ b ☐ c ☐	

E. The (proposed) conservatee's periods of impairment from the deficits indicated in items 6A–6D

(1) ☐ do NOT vary substantially in frequency, severity, or duration.

(2) ☐ do vary substantially in frequency, severity, or duration *(explain; continue on Attachment 6E if necessary):*

F. ☐ *(Optional)* Other information regarding my evaluation of the (proposed) conservatee's mental function (e.g., diagnosis, symptomatology, and other impressions) is ☐ stated below ☐ stated in Attachment 6F.

ABILITY TO CONSENT TO MEDICAL TREATMENT

7. Based on the information above, it is my opinion that the (proposed) conservatee

a. ☐ has the capacity to give informed consent to any form of medical treatment. This opinion is limited to medical consent capacity.

b. ☐ lacks the capacity to give informed consent to any form of medical treatment because he or she is *either* (1) unable to respond knowingly and intelligently regarding medical treatment *or* (2) unable to participate in a treatment decision by means of a rational thought process, *or both.* The deficits in the mental functions described in item 6 above significantly impair the (proposed) conservatee's ability to understand and appreciate the consequences of medical decisions. This opinion is limited to medical consent capacity.

(Declarant must initial here if item 7b applies: _____.)

8. Number of pages attached: _____

I declare under penalty of perjury under the laws of the State of California that the foregoing is true and correct.

Date:

▶

_____
(TYPE OR PRINT NAME)

_____
(SIGNATURE OF DECLARANT)

GC-335 [Rev. January 1, 2004]	**CAPACITY DECLARATION—CONSERVATORSHIP**	Page 3 of 3

Guardianship, Conservatorship and the Law

APPENDIX 7:
PETITION FOR APPOINTMENT OF
STANDBY GUARDIAN

F.C.A;§. 661
S.C.P.A.§§ 1704,1726

Form 6-8
(Petition for Appointment
of Standby Guardian)
1/2001

FAMILY COURT OF THE STATE OF NEW YORK
COUNTY OF
....

Proceeding for the Appointment of a
Standby Guardian of the Person

Docket No.

of

_____, a Minor
....

PETITION
(Appointment of
Standby Guardian)

TO THE FAMILY COURT:

The Petitioner respectfully alleges to this Court that:

1. The name and domicile of the Petitioner and relationship of the Petitioner to
the child who is the subject of this proceeding, are as follows:

Name:
Relationship to child [check applicable box]:
      ☐ mother   ☐ father   ☐ guardian   ☐ legal custodian   ☐ primary caretaker
Address [Include street, city, village or town, county and state]:

2. The name, date of birth and domicile of the child who is the subject of this proceeding are as
follows:

Name:
Date of Birth:
Address: [Including street, city, village or town, county and state]

3. The subject child (is)(is not) a Native American child subject to the Indian Child Welfare Act of 1978 (25 U.S.C. §§ 1901-1963).

4. The residence of the child and name and relationship of the person(s) with whom the child resides are as follows:

Person with whom child resides [specify name]:
Relationship to child [check applicable box]:
    ☐ mother   ☐ father   ☐ guardian   ☐ legal custodian   ☐ primary caretaker
Address [Include street, city, village or town, county and state]:

5. This petition seeks appointment of a Standby Guardian of the person of the child who is the

Form 6-8 page 2

subject of this proceeding, to become effective upon the petitioner's (incapacity) (death) (incapacity or death, whichever occurs first).[1]

6. On information and belief, petitioner suffers from a progressively chronic or fatal illness. The source of information and basis for belief are:

7. The religion of the child is

8. The names, relationship and post office addresses of the child's parent(s), the name and address of the person(s) with whom the child resides, if other than the parent(s), to whom process should issue; and such other persons concerning whom the court is required to have information, are as follows: (If a parent is deceased, so allege)

Relationship   Name   Post Office Address
Mother:

Father:

Person with whom
Child resides, if
other than parents:

Other:[2]

9. To protect and preserve the legal rights of the child, it is necessary that some proper person be duly appointed the Standby Guardian of (his)(her) person, because:

10. (Upon information and belief) No Guardian pursuant to Section 383-c, 384 or 384-b of the Social Services Law, or Standby Guardian pursuant to section 1726 of the Surrogate's Court Procedure Act, has been previously appointed for the child except [specify]:

11. (a). Petitioner (has)(does not have) knowledge that the person nominated to be a

---

[1] S.C.P.A. Section 1726(3)(I); delete inapplicable provisions.

[2] Include Mental Hygiene Legal Services if child is a mentally retarded or developmentally disabled person admitted to a facility.

standby guardian herein is the subject of an indicated report, as such term is defined in Section 412 of the Social Services Law, filed with the statewide register of child abuse and maltreatment pursuant to Title Six of Article Six of the Social Services Law. If so, specify date, status and circumstances to the extent known:

(b). Petitioner (has)(does not have) knowledge that the person nominated to be a standby guardian] herein is the subject of or the respondent in a child protective proceeding commenced under Article Ten of the Family Court Act. If so, specify whether proceeding resulted in an order finding that the child is an abused or neglected child, date and status to the extent known:

(c). Petitioner (has)(does not have) knowledge that an Order of Protection or Temporary Order of Protection (has)(has not) been issued against the person nominated to be a guardian herein in any criminal, matrimonial or Family Court proceeding(s). If such an order has been issued, specify the court, docket or index number, date of order, expiration date or order, next court date and status of case to the extent known:

12 (a). The following adults aged 18 or older reside with the proposed guardian:

Name   Relationship, if any, to Child   Date of Birth

(b). Upon information and belief, (none of the above adults) (the following adult(s)[specify]:
) (is)(are) the subject of an
indicated report, as such term is defined in Section 412 of the Social Services Law, filed with the statewide register of child abuse and maltreatment pursuant to Title Six of Article Six of the Social Services Law. If so, specify date, status and circumstances to the extent known:

(c). Upon information and belief, (none of the above adults) (the following adult(s)[specify]:
) (has) (have) been the subject of or the respondent in a child
protective proceeding commenced under Article 10 of the Family Court Act. If so, specify whether proceeding resulted in an order finding that the child is an abused or neglected child, date and status to the extent known:

(d). Upon information and belief, an Order of Protection or Temporary Order of Protection (has)(has not) been issued against any of the above adults in any criminal, matrimonial or Family Court proceeding(s). If such an order has been issued, specify the adult against whom the order was issued, the court that issued the order, docket number, date of order, expiration date of order, next court date and status of case to the extent known:

13.   , residing at   , whose

Form 6-8 page 4

religion is   would be a suitable and proper person to be appointed
Standby Guardian of the person of the Child, in that:

14. Attached hereto is the consent of the proposed Standby Guardian to being appointed Standby
Guardian of the person of the child.

(15. [Delete if inapplicable]: The parent(s) of the child, although living, should not be appointed
Standby Guardian of the person of the child because:

).

16. There are no persons interested in this proceeding other than those here in above mentioned.

17. No prior application has been made to any court for the relief herein requested.

WHEREFORE, Petitioner respectfully requests that an order be entered appointing   [specify]:
as Standby Guardian of the person of the child upon Petitioner's death (or incapacity,
whichever occurs first). [Delete if inapplicable. *See* S.C.P.A. §1726(3)].

Dated:

_____
Signature of Petitioner

_____
Print or type name

_____
Signature of Attorney, if any

_____
Attorney's Name (Print or Type)

_____
_____
Attorney's Address and Telephone Number

<u>VERIFICATION</u>

STATE OF NEW YORK   )
) ss.:
COUNTY OF   )
, being duly sworn, says that b(s)he is the Petitioner in the above-named proceeding and that the
foregoing petition is true to (his)(her) own knowledge, except as to matters therein stated to be alleged on
information and belief and as to those matters (s)he believes it to be true.

_____
Petitioner

Sworn to before me this

APPENDIX 8:
PETITION FOR APPOINTMENT
OF CONSERVATOR

GC-310

ATTORNEY OR PARTY WITHOUT ATTORNEY *(Name, State Bar number, and address)*:	*FOR COURT USE ONLY*
TELEPHONE NO.: FAX NO. *(Optional)*:	
E-MAIL ADDRESS *(Optional)*:	
ATTORNEY FOR *(Name)*:	

SUPERIOR COURT OF CALIFORNIA, COUNTY OF
   STREET ADDRESS:
   MAILING ADDRESS:
   CITY AND ZIP CODE:
   BRANCH NAME:

CONSERVATORSHIP OF

(Name):

(PROPOSED) CONSERVATEE

PETITION FOR APPOINTMENT OF ☐ **SUCCESSOR** **PROBATE CONSERVATOR OF THE** ☐ **PERSON** ☐ **ESTATE** ☐ **Limited Conservatorship**	CASE NUMBER:
	HEARING DATE AND TIME: DEPT.:

1. **Petitioner** *(name)*:   **requests that**

   a. *(Name)*:   *(Telephone)*:
      (Address):

   be appointed ☐ successor ☐ conservator ☐ limited conservator
   of the PERSON of the (proposed) conservatee and Letters issue upon qualification.

   b. *(Name)*:   *(Telephone)*:
      (Address):

   be appointed ☐ successor ☐ conservator ☐ limited conservator
   of the ESTATE of the (proposed) conservatee and Letters issue upon qualification.

   c. (1) ☐ bond not be required ☐ because the proposed ☐ successor conservator is a corporate fiduciary
         or an exempt government agency. ☐ for the reasons stated in Attachment 1c.

      (2) ☐ bond be fixed at: $ to be furnished by an authorized surety company or as otherwise provided
         by law. *(Specify reasons in Attachment 1c if the amount is different from the minimum required by Probate Code
         section 2320.)*

      (3) ☐ $ in deposits in a blocked account be allowed. Receipts will be filed. *(Specify institution and
         location)*:

d. ☐ orders authorizing independent exercise of powers under Probate Code section 2590 be granted.
Granting the proposed ☐ successor conservator of the estate powers to be exercised independently under Probate Code section 2590 would be to the advantage and benefit and in the best interest of the conservatorship estate. *(Specify orders, powers, and reasons in Attachment 1d.)*

e. ☐ orders relating to the capacity of the (proposed) conservatee under Probate Code section 1873 or 1901 be granted. *(Specify orders, facts, and reasons in Attachment 1e.)*

f. ☐ orders relating to the powers and duties of the proposed ☐ successor conservator of the person under Probate Code sections 2351–2358 be granted. *(Specify orders, facts, and reasons in Attachment 1f.)*

g. ☐ the (proposed) conservatee be adjudged to lack the capacity to give informed consent for medical treatment or healing by prayer and that the proposed ☐ successor conservator of the person be granted the powers specified in Probate Code section 2355. *(Complete item 9 on page 5.)*

Do NOT use this form for a temporary conservatorship.

Form Adopted for Mandatory Use
Judicial Council of California
GC-310 [Rev. January 1, 2006]

PETITION FOR APPOINTMENT OF PROBATE CONSERVATOR
(Probate—Guardianships and Conservatorships)

Probate Code, §§ 1820, 1821,
2680–2682
www.courtinfo.ca.gov

GC-310

CONSERVATORSHIP OF *(Name)*:	CASE NUMBER:
CONSERVATEE	

1. h. ☐ *(for limited conservatorship only)* orders relating to the powers and duties of the proposed ☐ successor *
limited conservator of the person under Probate Code section 2351.5 be granted.
(Specify orders, powers, and duties in Attachment 1h and complete item 1j.)

   i. ☐ *(for limited conservatorship only)* orders relating to the powers and duties of the proposed ☐ successor *
limited conservator of the estate under Probate Code section 1830(b) be granted.
(Specify orders, powers, and duties in Attachment 1i and complete item 1j.)

   j. ☐ *(for limited conservatorship only)* orders limiting the civil and legal rights of the (proposed) limited conservatee be granted.
(Specify limitations in Attachment 1j.)

   k. ☐ orders related to dementia placement or treatment as specified in the *Attachment Requesting Special Orders Regarding
Dementia* (form GC-313) under Probate Code section 2356.5 be granted. A *Capacity Declaration—Conservatorship*
(form GC-335) and *Dementia Attachment to Capacity Declaration—Conservatorship* (form GC-335A), executed by a
licensed physician or by a licensed psychologist acting within the scope of his or her licensure with at least two years
experience diagnosing dementia, ☐ are filed herewith. ☐ will be filed before the hearing.

   ☐ *(appointment of successor conservator only)* will not be filed because an order relating to dementia placement or
treatment was filed on *(date):* _____ . That order has neither expired by its terms nor been revoked.

   l. ☐ other orders be granted. *(Specify in Attachment 1l.)*

2. **(Proposed) conservatee** is *(name)*:
   (Present address):

   (Telephone):

3. a. ☐ **Jurisdictional facts** *(initial appointment only)*: The proposed conservatee has no conservator in California and is a
   (1) ☐ resident of California and
      (a) ☐ a resident of this county.
      (b) ☐ not a resident of this county, but commencement of the conservatorship in this county is in the best
          interests of the proposed conservatee. *(Specify reasons in Attachment 3a.)*
   (2) ☐ nonresident of California but
      (a) ☐ is temporarily living in this county, or
      (b) ☐ has property in this county, or
      (c) ☐ commencement of the conservatorship in this county is in the best interest of the proposed
          conservatee. *(Specify reasons in Attachment 3a.)*

   b. **Petitioner**
   (1) ☐ is ☐ is not a **creditor** or an agent of a creditor of the (proposed) conservatee.
   (2) ☐ is ☐ is not a **debtor** or an agent of a debtor of the (proposed) conservatee.

   c. **Proposed** ☐ **successor conservator** is *(check all that apply)*:
   (1) ☐ a nominee. (Affix *nomination as Attachment 3c.)*
   (2) ☐ the spouse of the (proposed) conservatee.
   (3) ☐ the domestic partner or former domestic partner of the (proposed) conservatee.
   (4) ☐ a relative of the (proposed) conservatee as *(specify relationship)*:
   (5) ☐ a bank ☐ other entity authorized to conduct the business of a trust company.
   (6) ☐ a nonprofit charitable corporation that meets the requirements of Probate Code section 2104.
   (7) ☐ a private professional conservator, as defined in Probate Code section 2341, who has filed with the court the
       information statement required by Probate Code section 2342.
   (8) (a) ☐ registered with the Statewide Registry of Private Conservators, Guardians, and Trustees maintained by the
       California Department of Justice under Probate Code sections 2850–2855. The current registration declaration
       on file will expire on *(date)*:
       (b) ☐ exempt from statewide registration under Probate Code section *(specify)*:
       (Explain basis for exemption in Attachment 3c.)
   (9) ☐ other *(specify)*:

   * See Item 5b on page 3.

PETITION FOR APPOINTMENT OF PROBATE CONSERVATOR
(Probate—Guardianships and Conservatorships)

GC-310

CONSERVATORSHIP OF *(Name):*	CASE NUMBER:
CONSERVATEE	

3. d. **Petitioner** is

    (1) ☐ the (proposed) conservatee.
    (2) ☐ the spouse of the (proposed) conservatee.
    (3) ☐ the domestic partner or former domestic partner of the (proposed) conservatee.
    (4) ☐ a relative of the (proposed) conservatee as *(specify relationship):*
    (5) ☐ a bank ☐ other entity authorized to conduct the business of a trust company.
    (6) ☐ a state or local public entity, officer, or employee.
    (7) ☐ an interested person or friend of the (proposed) conservatee.
    (8) ☐ the proposed ☐ successor conservator.
    (9) ☐ the guardian of the proposed conservatee.

   e. **Character and estimated value of the property of the estate** *(complete items (1) or (2) and (3), (4), and (5)):*

    (1) ☐ *(For appointment of successor conservator only, if complete Inventory and Appraisal filed by predecessor):*
        Personal property: $, per Inventory and Appraisal filed in this proceeding on
        (specify dates of filing of all inventories and appraisals):

    (2) ☐ Estimated value of personal property: $
    (3) Annual gross income from
       (a) real property: $
       (b) personal property: $
       (c) pensions: $
       (d) wages: $
       (e) public assistance benefits: $
       (f) other: $

    (4) **Total** of (1) or (2) and (3): $
    (5) Real property: $
       (a) ☐ per Inventory and Appraisal identified in item (1).
       (b) ☐ estimated value.

4. **(Proposed) conservatee**

   a. ☐ is ☐ is not a patient in or on leave of absence from a state institution under the jurisdiction of the California Department of Mental Health or the California Department of Developmental Services *(specify state institution):*

   b. ☐ is receiving or entitled to receive ☐ is neither receiving nor entitled to receive benefits from the U.S. Department of Veterans Affairs *(estimate amount of monthly benefit payable):* $
   c. ☐ is ☐ is not able to complete an affidavit of voter registration.

5. a. ☐ **Proposed conservatee** *(initial appointment of conservator only)*
    (1) ☐ is an adult.
    (2) ☐ will be an adult on the effective date of the order *(date):*
    (3) ☐ is a married minor.
    (4) ☐ is a minor whose marriage has been dissolved.

   b. ☐ **Vacancy in office of conservator** *(appointment of successor conservator only. A petition for appointment of a limited conservator after the death of a predecessor is a petition for initial appointment. (Prob. Code, § 1860.5(a)(1).)*
    There is a vacancy in the office of conservator of the ☐ person ☐ estate for the reasons ☐ specified in Attachment 5b. ☐ specified below.

PETITION FOR APPOINTMENT OF PROBATE CONSERVATOR
(Probate—Guardianships and Conservatorships)

GC-310

CONSERVATORSHIP OF *(Name):*	CASE NUMBER:
CONSERVATEE	

5. c. **(Proposed) conservatee** requires a conservator and is

    (1) ☐ unable to properly provide for his or her personal needs for physical health, food, clothing, or shelter.
        Supporting facts are ☐ specified in Attachment 5c(1) ☐ as follows:

    (2) ☐ substantially unable to manage his or her financial resources or to resist fraud or undue influence.
        Supporting facts are ☐ specified in Attachment 5c(2) ☐ as follows:

Guardianship, Conservatorship and the Law   **101**

GC-310

CONSERVATORSHIP OF *(Name):*	CASE NUMBER:
CONSERVATEE	

5. d. ☐ **(Proposed) conservatee** voluntarily requests the appointment of a ☐ successor conservator. *(Specify facts showing good cause in Attachment 5(d).)*

    e. ☐ *Confidential Supplemental Information* (form GC-312) is filed with this petition. *(Initial appointment of conservator only. All petitioners must file this form except banks and other entities authorized to do business as a trust company.)*

    f. **(Proposed) conservatee** ☐ is ☐ is not developmentally disabled as defined in Probate Code section 1420. Petitioner is aware of the requirements of Probate Code section 1827.5. *(Specify the nature and degree of the alleged disability in Attachment 5f).*

6. ☐ **Petitioner or proposed** ☐ **successor conservator is the spouse of the (proposed) conservatee.** *(If this statement is true, you must answer a or b.)*

    a. ☐ The (proposed) conservatee's spouse is not a party to any action or proceeding against the (proposed) conservatee for legal separation, dissolution of marriage, annulment, or adjudication of nullity of their marriage.

    b. ☐ Although the (proposed) conservatee's spouse is a party to an action or proceeding against the (proposed) conservatee for legal separation, dissolution, annulment, or adjudication of nullity of their marriage, or has obtained a judgment in one of these proceedings, it is in the best interest of the (proposed) conservatee that:

        (1) ☐ a ☐ successor conservator be appointed.

        (2) ☐ the spouse be appointed as the ☐ successor conservator.

    (If you checked item 6b(1) or (2) or both, specify the facts and reasons in Attachment 6b.)

7. ☐ **Petitioner or proposed** ☐ **successor conservator is the domestic partner or former domestic partner of the (proposed) conservatee.** *(If this statement is true, you must answer a or b.):*

    a. ☐ The domestic partner of the (proposed) conservatee has not terminated and does not intend to terminate the domestic partnership.

    b. ☐ Although the domestic partner or former domestic partner of the (proposed) conservatee intends to terminate or has terminated the domestic partnership, it is in the best interest of the (proposed) conservatee that:

        (1) ☐ a ☐ successor conservator be appointed.

        (2) ☐ the domestic partner or former domestic partner be appointed as the ☐ successor conservator.

    (If you checked item 7b(1) or (2) or both, specify the facts and reasons in Attachment 7b.)

8. **(Proposed) conservatee** *(check all that apply):*

    a. ☐ will attend the hearing AND ☐ is the petitioner ☐ is not the petitioner AND ☐ has ☐ has not nominated the proposed ☐ successor conservator.

    b. ☐ *(initial appointment of conservator only):* is able but unwilling to attend the hearing AND ☐ does ☐ does not wish to contest the establishment of a conservatorship, ☐ does ☐ does not object to the proposed conservator, AND ☐ does ☐ does not prefer that another person act as conservator.

    c. ☐ *(initial appointment of conservator only):* is unable to attend the hearing because of medical inability. A *Capacity Declaration—Conservatorship* (form GC–335), executed by a licensed medical practitioner or an accredited religious practitioner ☐ is filed with this petition. ☐ will be filed before the hearing.

    d. ☐ *(initial appointment of conservator only):* is not the petitioner, is out of state, and will not attend the hearing.

    e. ☐ *(appointment of successor conservator only):* will not attend the hearing.

9. ☐ **Medical treatment of (proposed) conservatee**

    a. There is no form of medical treatment for which the (proposed) conservatee has the capacity to give an informed consent.

    b. A *Capacity Declaration—Conservatorship* (form GC–335) executed by a licensed physician or by a licensed psychologist acting within the scope of his or her licensure, stating that the (proposed) conservatee lacks the capacity to give informed consent for any form of medical treatment and giving reasons and the factual basis for this conclusion, ☐ is filed with this petition. ☐ will be filed before the hearing. ☐ will not be filed for the reason stated in c.

    c. ☐ *(appointment of successor conservator only)* The conservatee's incapacity to consent to any form of medical treatment was determined by order filed in this matter on *(date):*
    That order has neither expired by its terms nor been revoked.

    d. (Proposed) conservatee ☐ is ☐ is not an adherent of a religion that relies on prayer alone for healing, as defined in Probate Code section 2355(b).

PETITION FOR APPOINTMENT OF PROBATE CONSERVATOR
(Probate—Guardianships and Conservatorships)

GC-310

CONSERVATORSHIP OF (Name):	CASE NUMBER:
CONSERVATEE	

10. ☐ **Temporary conservatorship**
    Filed with this petition is a *Petition for Appointment of Temporary Guardian or Conservator* (form GC-110).

11. **(Proposed) conservatee's relatives**
    The names, residence addresses, and relationships of the spouse or registered domestic partner and the second-degree relatives of the (proposed) conservatee (his or her parents, grandparents, children, grandchildren, and brothers and sisters), so far as known to petitioner, are

    a. ☐ listed below.
    b. ☐ not known, or none are now living, so the (proposed) conservatee's deemed relatives under Probate Code section 1821(b)(1)–(4) are listed below.

    Name and relationship to conservatee | Residence address
    (1)

    (2)

    (3)

    (4)

    (5)

    (6)

    ☐ Continued on Attachment 11.

12. ☐ **Confidential conservator screening form**
    Submitted with this petition is a *Confidential Conservator Screening Form* (form GC-314) completed and signed by the proposed ☐ successor conservator. *(Required for all proposed conservators except banks and trust companies.)*

13. ☐ **Court investigator**
    Filed with this petition is a proposed *Order Appointing Court Investigator* (form GC-330).

14. Number of pages attached: _____

Date:

▶ _____
(TYPE OR PRINT NAME OF ATTORNEY FOR PETITIONER)   (SIGNATURE OF ATTORNEY FOR PETITIONER)

(All petitioners must also sign (Prob. Code, § 1020; Cal. Rules of Court, rule 7.103).)

I declare under penalty of perjury under the laws of the State of California that the foregoing is true and correct.

Date:

▶ _____
(TYPE OR PRINT NAME OF PETITIONER)   (SIGNATURE OF PETITIONER)

▶ _____
(TYPE OR PRINT NAME OF PETITIONER)   (SIGNATURE OF PETITIONER)

GC-310 [Rev. January 1, 2006]   **PETITION FOR APPOINTMENT OF PROBATE CONSERVATOR**   Page 6 of 6
                                        (Probate—Guardianships and Conservatorships)

APPENDIX 9:
PETITION FOR APPOINTMENT OF
TEMPORARY CONSERVATOR

GC-110

ATTORNEY OR PARTY WITHOUT ATTORNEY (Name, State Bar number, and address):	FOR COURT USE ONLY
TELEPHONE NO.: FAX NO. (Optional):	
E-MAIL ADDRESS (Optional):	
ATTORNEY FOR (Name):	

SUPERIOR COURT OF CALIFORNIA, COUNTY OF
STREET ADDRESS:
MAILING ADDRESS:
CITY AND ZIP CODE:
BRANCH NAME:

TEMPORARY ☐ GUARDIANSHIP ☐ CONSERVATORSHIP OF *(Name):*

☐ MINOR ☐ CONSERVATEE

PETITION FOR APPOINTMENT OF TEMPORARY ☐ **GUARDIAN** ☐ **CONSERVATOR** ☐ **Person*** ☐ **Estate***	CASE NUMBER:

1. **Petitioner** *(name each):*

requests that

  a. *(Name):*
    (Address and
    telephone number):
    be appointed temporary ☐ guardian ☐ conservator of the PERSON of the
    ☐ minor ☐ proposed conservatee   and Letters issue upon qualification.

  b. *(Name):*
    (Address and
    telephone number):
    be appointed temporary ☐ guardian ☐ conservator of the ESTATE of the
    ☐ minor ☐ proposed conservatee   and Letters issue upon qualification.

  c. (1) ☐ bond not be required because petition is for a temporary guardianship or conservatorship of the person only.
    (2) ☐ bond not be required for the reasons stated in Attachment 1c.
    (3) ☐ $ bond be fixed. It will be furnished by an admitted surety insurer or as otherwise provided by law.
       (Specify reasons in Attachment 1c if the amount is different from maximum required by Probate Code section 2320.)
    (4) ☐ $ in deposits in a blocked account be allowed. Receipts will be filed.
       (Specify institution and location):

d. ☐ the powers specified in Attachment 1d be granted in addition to the powers provided by law.

e. ☐ an order be granted dispensing with notice to the ☐ minor ☐ proposed conservatee ☐ minor's mother ☐ minor's father ☐ other person having a visitation order for the reasons stated in Attachment 1e.
(Identify each by name and relationship.)

f. ☐ other orders be granted *(specify in Attachment 1f).*

2. The ☐ minor ☐ proposed conservatee is *(name):*
Current address: Current telephone no.:

3. The ☐ minor ☐ proposed conservatee requires a temporary ☐ guardian ☐ conservator to ☐ provide for temporary care, maintenance, and support ☐ protect property from loss or injury because
(facts are ☐ *specified in Attachment 3* ☐ *as follows):*

You MAY use this form or form GC-110(P) for a temporary guardianship of the person. You MUST use this form for a temporary guardianship of the estate or the person and estate or for a temporary conservatorship.   **Page 1 of 2**

Form Adopted for Mandatory and Alternative Mandatory Use Instead of Form GC-110(P) Judicial Council of California GC-110 [Rev. January 1, 2007]	**PETITION FOR APPOINTMENT OF TEMPORARY GUARDIAN OR CONSERVATOR** (Probate—Guardianships and Conservatorships)	Probate Code, § 2250; Cal. Rules of Court, rule 7.101 *www.courtinfo.ca.gov*

GC-110

TEMPORARY ☐ GUARDIANSHIP ☐ CONSERVATORSHIP OF *(Name):*	CASE NUMBER:
☐ MINOR ☐ CONSERVATEE	

4. Temporary ☐ guardianship ☐ conservatorship is required
   a. ☐ pending the hearing on the petition for appointment of a general ☐ guardian ☐ conservator.
   b. ☐ pending the appeal under Probate Code section 1301.
   c. ☐ during the suspension of powers of the ☐ guardian ☐ conservator.

5. ☐ *(Complete if a temporary guardianship or conservatorship of the estate or person and estate is requested.)*
    Character and estimated value of the property of the estate:
   a. Personal property: $
   b. Annual gross income from all sources, including real and
      personal property, wages, pensions, and public benefits: $ _____
   c. **Total:** $ _____

6. ☐ **Change of Residence of Proposed Conservatee**
   a. ☐ Petitioner requests that the residence of the proposed conservatee be changed to *(address):*

      The proposed conservatee will suffer irreparable harm if his or her residence is not changed as requested and no means
      less restrictive of the proposed conservatee's liberty will suffice to prevent the harm because *(precise reasons are*
      ☐ *specified in Attachment 6a* ☐ *as follows):*

   b. ☐ The proposed conservatee must be removed from the State of California to permit the performance of the following non
      psychiatric medical treatment essential to the proposed conservatee's physical survival. The proposed conservatee
      consents to this medical treatment.
      (Facts and place of treatment are ☐ *specified in Attachment 6b* ☐ *as follows):*

   c. *(Change of residence only)* The proposed conservatee
     (1) ☐ will attend the hearing.
     (2) ☐ is able but unwilling to attend the hearing, does not wish to contest the establishment of a conservatorship, does not
           object to the proposed conservator, and does not prefer that another person act as conservator.
     (3) ☐ is unable to attend the hearing because of medical inability. An affidavit or certificate of a licensed medical
           practitioner or an accredited religious practitioner is affixed as Attachment 6c.
     (4) ☐ is not the petitioner, is out of state, and will not attend the hearing.
   d. ☐ *(Change of residence only)* Filed with this petition is a proposed *Order Appointing Court Investigator* (form GC-330).

7. Petitioner believes the ☐ minor ☐ proposed conservatee ☐ will ☐ will not attend the hearing.

8. All attachments to this form are incorporated by this reference as though placed here in this form. There are _____ pages
   attached to this form.

Date: ▶ _____
                                    (SIGNATURE OF ATTORNEY*)

* (Signature of all petitioners also required (Prob. Code, § 1020).)

I declare under penalty of perjury under the laws of the State of California that the foregoing is true and correct.

Date: ▶ _____

_____   ▶ _____
     (TYPE OR PRINT NAME)   (SIGNATURE OF PETITIONER)

_____   ▶ _____
     (TYPE OR PRINT NAME)   (SIGNATURE OF PETITIONER)

GC-110 [Rev. January 1, 2007]   **PETITION FOR APPOINTMENT OF**   Page 2 of 2
                          TEMPORARY GUARDIAN OR CONSERVATOR
                          (Probate—Guardianships and Conservatorships)

APPENDIX 10:
LETTERS OF TEMPORARY
CONSERVATORSHIP

GC-150

ATTORNEY OR PARTY WITHOUT ATTORNEY *(Name, state bar number, and address)*: After recording return to: TELEPHONE NO.: FAX NO. *(Optional)*: E-MAIL ADDRESS *(Optional)*: ATTORNEY FOR *(Name)*:	

SUPERIOR COURT OF CALIFORNIA, COUNTY OF
STREET ADDRESS:
MAILING ADDRESS:
CITY AND ZIP CODE:
BRANCH NAME:

TEMPORARY ☐ GUARDIANSHIP ☐ CONSERVATORSHIP
OF *(Name)*:

FOR RECORDER'S USE ONLY

☐ MINOR ☐ CONSERVATEE

CASE NUMBER:

LETTERS OF TEMPORARY ☐ **GUARDIANSHIP** ☐ **CONSERVATORSHIP**
☐ **Person** ☐ **Estate**

FOR COURT USE ONLY

LETTERS

1. *(Name)*:
 is appointed temporary ☐ guardian ☐ conservator of the ☐ person
 ☐ estate of *(name)*:

2. ☐ Other powers have been granted or restrictions imposed on the temporary
 ☐ guardian ☐ conservator as ☐ specified below
 ☐ specified in Attachment 2.

3. These *Letters* shall expire
 a. ☐ on *(date)*: or upon earlier issuance of *Letters* to a general
 guardian or conservator.
 b. ☐ other date *(specify)*:

4. ☐ The temporary ☐ guardian ☐ conservator is not authorized to take possession of money or any other property
 without a specific court order.

---

5. Number of pages attached: _____

WITNESS, clerk of the court, with seal of the court affixed.

(SEAL)	Date:
	Clerk, by
	_____
	(DEPUTY)

AFFIRMATION

I solemnly affirm that I will perform the duties of temporary ☐ guardian ☐ conservator according to law.

Executed on *(date)*:

at *(place)*: _____ , California.

▶ _____
(SIGNATURE OF APPOINTEE)

(SEAL)	WITNESS, clerk of the court, with seal of the court affixed.
	Date:
	Clerk, by
	_____
	(DEPUTY)

CERTIFICATION

I certify that this document and any attachments is a correct copy of the original on file in my office, and that the *Letters* issued to the person appointed above have not been revoked, annulled, or set aside and are still in full force and effect.

Form Approved for Mandatory Use
Judicial Council of California
GC-150 [Rev. January 1, 2003]

**LETTERS OF TEMPORARY
GUARDIANSHIP OR CONSERVATORSHIP**

Probate Code, § 2250 et seq.;
Code of Civil Procedure, § 2015.6

APPENDIX 11:
ORDER APPOINTING TEMPORARY CONSERVATOR

ATTORNEY OR PARTY WITHOUT ATTORNEY *(Name, state bar number, and address)*: TELEPHONE AND FAX NOS.:	*FOR COURT USE ONLY*
ATTORNEY FOR *(Name)*:	

SUPERIOR COURT OF CALIFORNIA, COUNTY OF
STREET ADDRESS:
MAILING ADDRESS:
CITY AND ZIP CODE:
BRANCH NAME:

TEMPORARY ☐ GUARDIANSHIP ☐ CONSERVATORSHIP OF THE
☐ PERSON ☐ ESTATE OF *(Name)*:
☐ MINOR ☐ CONSERVATEE

ORDER APPOINTING TEMPORARY ☐ **GUARDIAN** ☐ **CONSERVATOR**	CASE NUMBER:

WARNING: THIS APPOINTMENT IS NOT EFFECTIVE UNTIL LETTERS HAVE ISSUED.

1. The petition for appointment of a temporary ☐ guardian ☐ conservator came on for hearing as follows *(check boxes c and d to indicate personal presence)*:
   a. Judge *(name)*:
   b. Hearing date: Time: ☐ Dept.: ☐ Room:
   c. ☐ Petitioner *(name)*:
      ☐ Attorney for petitioner *(name)*:
   d. ☐ Minor ☐ Conservatee *(name)*:
      Attorney for ☐ minor ☐ conservatee *(name)*:

THE COURT FINDS
2. a. ☐ Notice of time and place of hearing has been given as required by law.
   b. ☐ Notice of time and place of hearing ☐ has been ☐ should be dispensed with for *(names)*:

3. ☐ It is necessary that a temporary ☐ guardian ☐ conservator be appointed to ☐ provide for temporary care, maintenance, and support ☐ protect property from loss or injury.
   ☐ pending the hearing on the petition for appointment of a general ☐ guardian ☐ conservator.
   ☐ pending an appeal under Probate Code section 1301.
   ☐ during the suspension of powers of the ☐ guardian ☐ conservator.

4. ☐ To prevent irreparable harm, the residence of the conservatee must be changed. No means less restrictive of the conservatee's liberty will prevent irreparable harm.

5. ☐ The conservatee must be removed from the State of California to permit the performance of nonpsychiatric medical treatment essential to the conservatee's physical survival. The conservatee consents to this medical treatment.

6. ☐ The conservatee need not attend the hearing on change of residence or removal from the State of California.

THE COURT ORDERS

7. a. *(Name):*
   (Address):   *(Telephone):*

   is appointed temporary ☐ guardian ☐ conservator of the PERSON of
   (name):   and *Letters* shall issue upon qualification

(Continued on reverse)

Form Approved by the
Judicial Council of California
GC-140 [Rev. January 1, 1998]

**ORDER APPOINTING
TEMPORARY GUARDIAN OR CONSERVATOR**

Probate Code, §§ 2250-2254

TEMPORARY ☐ GUARDIANSHIP ☐ CONSERVATORSHIP OF *(Name)*: ☐ ☐ MINOR ☐ CONSERVATEE	CASE NUMBER:

7. b. *(Name)*:

   (Address):   *(Telephone)*:

   is appointed temporary ☐ guardian ☐ conservator   of the ESTATE of
   (name):   and *Letters* shall issue upon qualification.

8. ☐ Notice of hearing to the persons named in item 2b is dispensed with.

9. a. ☐ Bond is not required.
   b. ☐ Bond is fixed at: $ to be furnished by an authorized surety company or as otherwise provided by law.
   c. ☐ Deposits of: $ are ordered to be placed in a blocked account at *(specify institution and location)*:

   and receipts shall be filed. No withdrawals shall be made without a court order. ☐ Additional orders in Attachment 9c.
   d. ☐ The temporary ☐ guardian ☐ conservator   is not authorized to take possession of money or any other property without a specific court order.

10. ☐ The conservator is authorized to change the residence of the conservatee to *(address)*:

11. ☐ The conservator is authorized to remove the conservatee from the State of California to the following address to permit the performance of nonpsychiatric medical treatment essential to the conservatee's physical survival *(address)*:

12. ☐ The conservatee need not attend the hearing on change of residence or removal from the State of California.

13. ☐ In addition to the powers granted by law, the temporary conservator is granted other powers. These powers are specified ☐ in Attachment 13 ☐ below *(specify)*:

14. ☐ Other orders as specified in Attachment 14 are granted.

15. ☐ Unless modified by further order of the court, this order expires on *(date)*:

16. Number of boxes checked in items 8-15: _____

17. Number of pages attached: _____

Date: _____

                     _____
                     JUDGE OF THE SUPERIOR COURT
                     ☐ SIGNATURE FOLLOWS LAST ATTACHMENT

GC-140 [Rev. January 1, 1998] **ORDER APPOINTING TEMPORARY GUARDIAN OR CONSERVATOR** Page two

APPENDIX 12:
LETTERS OF CONSERVATORSHIP

GC-350

ATTORNEY OR PARTY WITHOUT ATTORNEY *(Name, state bar number, and address):*

After recording return to:

TELEPHONE NO.:
FAX NO. *(Optional):*
E-MAIL ADDRESS *(Optional):*
ATTORNEY FOR *(Name):*

SUPERIOR COURT OF CALIFORNIA, COUNTY OF

STREET ADDRESS:
MAILING ADDRESS:
CITY AND ZIP CODE:
BRANCH NAME:

CONSERVATORSHIP OF *(Name):*

FOR RECORDER'S USE ONLY

CONSERVATEE

CASE NUMBER:

LETTERS OF CONSERVATORSHIP
☐ **Person**   ☐ **Estate**   ☐ **Limited Conservatorship**

1. ☐ *(Name):* is the appointed
☐ conservator ☐ limited conservator of the ☐ person ☐ estate
of *(name):*

2. ☐ *(For conservatorship that was on December 31, 1980, a guardianship of an adult
or of the person of a married minor)* *(Name):*
was appointed the guardian of the ☐ person ☐ estate by order
dated *(specify):* and is now the conservator of
the ☐ person ☐ estate of *(name):*

3. ☐ Other powers have been granted or conditions imposed as follows:
 a. ☐ Exclusive authority to give consent for and to require the conservatee to
   receive medical treatment that the conservator in good faith based on
   medical advice determines to be necessary even if the conservatee
   objects, subject to the limitations stated in Probate Code section 2356.
  (1) ☐ This treatment shall be performed by an accredited practitioner
    of the religion whose tenets and practices call for reliance on
    prayer alone for healing of which the conservatee was an adherent prior to the establishment of the
    conservatorship.
  (2) ☐ *(If court order limits duration)* This medical authority terminates on *(date):*
 b. ☐ Authority to place conservatee in a care or nursing facility described in Probate Code section 2356.5(b).
 c. ☐ Authority to authorize the administration of medications appropriate for the care and treatment of dementia described
   in Probate Code section 2356.5(c).
 d. ☐ Powers to be exercised independently under Probate Code section 2590 as specified in Attachment 3d *(specify
   powers, restrictions, conditions, and limitations).*

FOR COURT USE ONLY

Guardianship, Conservatorship and the Law

e. ☐ Conditions relating to the care and custody of the property under Probate Code section 2402 as specified in Attachment 3e.

f. ☐ Conditions relating to the care, treatment, education, and welfare of the conservatee under Probate Code section 2358 as specified in Attachment 3f.

g. ☐ *(For limited conservatorship only)* Powers of the limited conservator of the person under Probate Code section 2351.5 as specified in Attachment 3g.

h. ☐ *(For limited conservatorship only)* Powers of the limited conservator of the estate under Probate Code section 1830(b) as specified in Attachment 3h.

i. ☐ Other *(specify):*

(SEAL)

4. ☐ The conservator is **not** authorized to take possession of money or any other property without a specific court order.

5. Number of pages attached: _____

WITNESS, clerk of the court, with seal of the court affixed.

Date:

Clerk, by _____, Deputy

Page 1 of 2

This form may be recorded as notice of the establishment of a conservatorship of the estate as provided in Probate Code section 1875.

Form Adopted for Mandatory Use
Judicial Council of California
GC-350 [Rev. January 1, 2003]

LETTERS OF CONSERVATORSHIP

Probate Code, § 1834

CONSERVATORSHIP OF *(Name)*:	CASE NUMBER:
CONSERVATEE	

LETTERS OF CONSERVATORSHIP

AFFIRMATION

I solemnly affirm that I will perform according to law the duties of ☐ conservator ☐ limited conservator.

Executed on *(date)*: , at *(place)*:

▶ _____

(SIGNATURE OF APPOINTEE)

CERTIFICATION

I certify that this document and any attachments is a correct copy of the original on file in my office, and that the letters issued to the person appointed above have not been revoked, annulled, or set aside, and are still in full force and effect.

Date: Clerk, by _____ , Deputy

(SEAL)

GC-350 [Rev. January 1, 2003] **LETTERS OF CONSERVATORSHIP** Page 2 of 2

APPENDIX 13:
ORDER APPOINTING CONSERVATOR

GC-340

ATTORNEY OR PARTY WITHOUT ATTORNEY *(Name, State Bar number, and address)*:	FOR COURT USE ONLY
TELEPHONE NO.:　　　　　　FAX NO. *(Optional)*: E-MAIL ADDRESS *(Optional)*: ATTORNEY FOR *(Name)*:	

SUPERIOR COURT OF CALIFORNIA, COUNTY OF
STREET ADDRESS:
MAILING ADDRESS:
CITY AND ZIP CODE:
BRANCH NAME:

CONSERVATORSHIP OF
(Name):

CONSERVATEE

ORDER APPOINTING ☐ **SUCCESSOR PROBATE CONSERVATOR OF THE** ☐ **PERSON** ☐ **ESTATE** ☐ **Limited Conservatorship**	CASE NUMBER:

WARNING: THIS APPOINTMENT IS NOT EFFECTIVE UNTIL LETTERS HAVE ISSUED.

1. The petition for appointment of ☐ successor　conservator came on for hearing as follows
   (check boxes c, d, e, and f or g to indicate personal presence):
   a.　Judicial Officer *(name)*:
   b.　Hearing date:　　　　　　Time:　　　　☐ Dept.:　　　　☐ Room:
   c.　☐ Petitioner *(name)*:
   d.　☐ Attorney for petitioner *(name)*:
   e.　☐ Attorney for ☐ person cited ☐ the conservatee on petition to appoint successor conservator:
   　　(Name):　　　　　　　　　　　　　　　　*(Telephone)*:
   　　(Address):

   f.　☐ Person cited was ☐ present. ☐ unable to attend. ☐ able but unwilling to attend. ☐ out of state.
   g.　☐ The conservatee on petition to appoint successor conservator was ☐ present. ☐ not present.

THE COURT FINDS

2. All notices required by law have been given.

3. *(Name)*:
   a.　☐ is unable properly to provide for his or her personal needs for physical health, food, clothing, or shelter.
   b.　☐ is substantially unable to manage his or her financial resources or to resist fraud or undue influence.

---

4. The conservatee
   a. ☐ is an adult.
   b. ☐ will be an adult on the effective date of this order.
   c. ☐ is a married minor.
   d. ☐ is a minor whose marriage has been dissolved.

5. ☐ There is no form of medical treatment for which the conservatee has the capacity to give an informed consent.
    ☐ The conservatee is an adherent of a religion defined in Probate Code section 2355(b).

6. ☐ Granting the ☐ successor conservator powers to be exercised independently under Probate Code section 2590 is to the advantage and benefit and in the best interest of the conservatorship estate.

7. ☐ The conservatee is not capable of completing an affidavit of voter registration.

8. ☐ The conservatee has dementia as defined in Probate Code section 2356.5, and the court finds all other facts required to make the orders specified in item 27.

Do NOT use this form for a temporary conservatorship.

Form Adopted for Mandatory Use
Judicial Council of California
GC-340 [Rev. January 1, 2006]

ORDER APPOINTING PROBATE CONSERVATOR
(Probate—Guardianships and Conservatorships)

Probate Code, §§ 1830, 2688
www.courtinfo.ca.gov

GC-340

CONSERVATORSHIP OF (Name):	CASE NUMBER:
CONSERVATEE	

9. ☐ Attorney (name): has been appointed by the court as legal counsel to represent the conservatee in these proceedings. The cost for representation is: $
   The conservatee has the ability to pay ☐ all ☐ none ☐ a portion of this sum (specify): $

10. ☐ The conservatee need not attend the hearing.

11. ☐ The appointed court investigator is (name):

   (Address and telephone):

12. ☐ (For limited conservatorship only) The limited conservatee is developmentally disabled as defined in Probate Code section 1420.

13. ☐ The ☐ successor conservator is a private professional conservator as defined by Probate Code section 2341 who has filed with the court the confidential statement required by Probate Code section 2342.

14. The ☐ successor conservator (check a or b):
   a. ☐ is currently registered with the Statewide Registry of Private Conservators, Guardians, and Trustees maintained by the California Department of Justice under Probate Code sections 2850–2855.
   b. ☐ is exempt from statewide registration under Probate Code sections 2850–2855.

15. (Either a, b, or c must be checked):
   a. ☐ The ☐ successor conservator is not the spouse of the conservatee.
   b. ☐ The ☐ successor conservator is the spouse of the conservatee and is not a party to an action or proceeding against the conservatee for legal separation, dissolution, annulment, or adjudication of nullity of their marriage.
   c. ☐ The ☐ successor conservator is the spouse of the conservatee and is a party to an action or proceeding against the conservatee for legal separation, dissolution, annulment, or adjudication of nullity of their marriage. It is in the best interests of the conservatee to appoint the spouse as ☐ successor conservator.

16. (Either a, b, or c must be checked):
   a. ☐ The ☐ successor conservator is not the domestic partner or former domestic partner of the conservatee.
   b. ☐ The ☐ successor conservator is the domestic partner of the conservatee and has neither terminated nor intends to terminate their domestic partnership.
   c. ☐ The ☐ successor conservator is the domestic partner or former domestic partner of the conservatee and intends to terminate or has terminated their domestic partnership. It is in the best interest of the conservatee to appoint the domestic partner or former domestic partner as ☐ successor conservator.

THE COURT ORDERS

17. a. (Name): (Telephone):
   (Address):

   is appointed ☐ successor ☐ conservator ☐ limited conservator of the PERSON of (name):
   and Letters of Conservatorship shall issue upon qualification.

   b. (Name): (Telephone):
   (Address):

   is appointed ☐ successor ☐ conservator ☐ limited conservator of the ESTATE of (name):
   and Letters of Conservatorship shall issue upon qualification.

18. ☐ The conservatee need not attend the hearing.

19. a. ☐ Bond is not required.
   b. ☐ Bond is fixed at: $ to be furnished by an authorized surety company or as otherwise provided by law.
   c. ☐ Deposits of: $ are ordered to be placed in a blocked account at (specify institution and location):

   and receipts shall be filed. No withdrawals shall be made without a court order.
   ☐ Additional orders in Attachment 19c.

   d. ☐ The ☐ successor conservator is not authorized to take possession of money or any other property without a specific court order.

GC-340 [Rev. January 1, 2006]

ORDER APPOINTING PROBATE CONSERVATOR
(Probate—Guardianships and Conservatorships)

Page 2 of 3

GC-340

CONSERVATORSHIP OF *(Name)*:	CASE NUMBER:
CONSERVATEE	

20. ☐ For legal services rendered, ☐ conservatee ☐ conservatee's estate ☐ parents of the minor ☐ minor's
estate shall pay to *(name)*: the sum of: $
☐ forthwith ☐ as follows *(specify terms, including any combination of payors)*:

☐ Continued in Attachment 20.

21. ☐ The conservatee is disqualified from voting.

22. ☐ The conservatee lacks the capacity to give informed consent for medical treatment and the ☐ successor
conservator of the person is granted the powers specified in Probate Code section 2355.
☐ The treatment shall be performed by an accredited practitioner of a religion as defined in Probate Code
section 2355(b).

23. ☐ The ☐ successor conservator of the estate is granted authorization under Probate Code section 2590 to exercise
independently the powers specified in Attachment 23 ☐ subject to the conditions provided.

24. ☐ Orders relating to the capacity of the conservatee under Probate Code sections 1873 or 1901 as specified in Attachment 24
are granted.

25. ☐ Orders relating to the powers and duties of the ☐ successor conservator of the person under
Probate Code sections 2351–2358 as specified in Attachment 25 are granted. *(Do not include orders under Probate
Code section 2356.5 relating to dementia.)*

26. ☐ Orders relating to the conditions imposed under Probate Code section 2402 on the ☐ successor conservator
of the estate as specified in Attachment 26 are granted.

27. ☐ a. ☐ The ☐ successor conservator of the person is granted authority to place the conservatee in a care or
nursing facility described in Probate Code section 2356.5(b).
    b. ☐ The ☐ successor conservator of the person is granted authority to authorize the administration of
medications appropriate for the care and treatment of dementia described in Probate Code section 2356.5(c).

28. ☐ Other orders as specified in Attachment 28 are granted.

29. ☐ The probate referee appointed is *(name and address)*:

30. ☐ *(For limited conservatorship only)* Orders relating to the powers and duties of the ☐ successor
limited conservator of the person under Probate Code section 2351.5 as specified in Attachment 30 are granted.

31. ☐ *(For limited conservatorship only)* Orders relating to the powers and duties of the ☐ successor
limited conservator of the estate under Probate Code section 1830(b) as specified in Attachment 31 are granted.

32. ☐ *(For limited conservatorship only)* Orders limiting the civil and legal rights of the limited conservatee as specified in
Attachment 32 are granted.

33. ☐ This order is effective on the ☐ date signed ☐ date minor attains majority *(specify)*:

34. Number of boxes checked in items 17–33: _____

35. Number of pages attached: _____

Date:

_____
JUDICIAL OFFICER
☐ SIGNATURE FOLLOWS LAST ATTACHMENT

ORDER APPOINTING PROBATE CONSERVATOR
(Probate—Guardianships and Conservatorships)

Guardianship, Conservatorship and the Law

APPENDIX 14:
WILL PROVISION APPOINTING
A GUARDIAN FOR MINOR CHILD

In the event that, upon my death, there is no living person who is entitled by law to the custody of my minor children, [NAMES AND DATES OF BIRTH OF CHILDREN], and who is available to assume such custody, I name [GUARDIAN'S NAME], presently residing at [GUARDIAN'S ADDRESS], as legal guardian of my aforementioned minor children, to serve without bond.

APPENDIX 15:
LIVING WILL

DECLARATION made this_____ day of_____, 20___.

I, [Name of Declarant], residing at [Address], being of sound mind, willfully and voluntarily make known my desire that my life shall not be artificially prolonged under the circumstances set forth below, and do hereby declare:

MEDICAL CONDITION

1. If at any time I should have a terminal or incurable condition caused by injury, disease, or illness, certified to be terminal or incurable by at least two physicians, which within reasonable medical judgment would cause my death, and where the application of life-sustaining procedures would serve only to artificially prolong the moment of my death, I direct that such procedures be withheld or withdrawn, and that I be permitted to die with dignity.

2. If at any time I experience irreversible brain injury, or a disease, illness, or condition that results in my being in a permanent, irreversible vegetative or comatose state, and such injury, disease, illness, or condition would preclude any cognitive, meaningful, or functional future existence, I direct my physicians and any other attending nursing or health care personnel to allow me to die with dignity, even if that requires the withdrawal or withholding of nutrition or hydration and my death will follow such withdrawal or withholding.

LIFE-SUSTAINING PROCEDURES

It is my expressed intent that the term "life-sustaining procedures" shall include not only medical or surgical procedures or interventions that utilize mechanical or other artificial means to sustain, restore, or supplant a vital function, but also shall include the placement, withdrawal, withholding, or maintenance of nasogastric tubes, gastrostomy, intravenous lines, or any other artificial, surgical, or invasive means for nutritional support and/or hydration.

"Life-sustaining procedures" shall not be interpreted to include the administration of medication or the performance of any medical procedure deemed necessary to provide routine care and comfort or alleviate pain.

RIGHT TO REFUSE TREATMENT

It is my intent and expressed desire that this Declaration shall be honored by my family, physicians, nurses, and any other attending health care personnel as the final expression of my constitutional and legal right to refuse medical or surgical treatment and to accept the consequences of such refusal. Any ambiguities, questions, or uncertainties that might arise in the reading, interpretation, or implementation of this Declaration shall be resolved in a manner to give complete expression to my legal right to refuse treatment and shall be construed as clear and convincing evidence of my intentions and desires.

REVOCATION OF PREVIOUSLY EXECUTED DOCUMENTS

I understand the full importance of this Declaration and I am emotionally and mentally competent to make this Declaration, and by my execution, I hereby revoke any previously executed health care declaration.

COPIES AND DISTRIBUTION

The original of this document is kept at [Address]. I have made (xx#) copies of this document. Numbered and signed copies have been provided to the following individuals or institutions: [List names, addresses and phone numbers of individuals and institutions].

Signed in the presence of the witnesses who have signed below this ____ day of _____, 20___ .

SIGNATURE LINE – DECLARANT

STATEMENT OF WITNESSES

I state this____ day of_____, 20__, under penalty of perjury, that the Declarant has identified himself/herself to me and that the Declarant signed or acknowledged this health care declaration in my presence.

I believe the Declarant to be of sound mind, and the Declarant has affirmed his/her awareness of the nature of this document and is signing it voluntarily and free from duress. The Declarant requested that I serve as a witness to his/her execution of this document.

I declare that I am not related to the Declarant by blood, marriage, or adoption and that to the best of my knowledge I am not entitled to any part of the estate of the Declarant on the death of the principal under a will or by operation of law.

I am not a provider of health or residential care, an employee of a provider of health or residential care, the operator of a community care facility, or an employee of an operator of a health care facility.

I declare that I have no claim against any portion of the estate of the Declarant upon his/her death, or any personal financial responsibility for the payment of Declarant's medical bills or any other of Declarant's obligations.

SIGNATURE LINE/ADDRESS/DATE – WITNESS #1

SIGNATURE LINE/ADDRESS/DATE – WITNESS #2

SIGNATURE LINE/ADDRESS/DATE – WITNESS #3

NOTARIAL ACKNOWLEDGMENT

BEFORE ME, the undersigned authority, on this day personally appeared [insert name of declarant], and [names of three witnesses], known to me to be the declarant and witnesses whose names are subscribed to the foregoing instrument in their respective capacities, and, all of said persons being by me duly sworn, [name of declarant] declared to me and to the said witnesses in my presence that said instrument is (his/her) Living Will, and that (he/she) had willingly and voluntarily made and executed it as (his/her) free act and deed for the purposes therein expressed.

@P = SUBSCRIBED AND SWORN TO BEFORE ME by the declarant, [insert name] and by the witnesses [insert names] this _____ day of _____, 20_____.

SIGNATURE LINE AND STAMP - NOTARY PUBLIC

APPENDIX 16:
TABLE OF STATE LIVING WILL STATUTES

STATE STATUTE	CITATION
Alabama—Natural Death Act	Alabama Code §§ 22-8A-1 et seq.
Alaska—Rights of the Terminally Ill Act	Alaska Statutes §§ 18.12.010
Arizona—Medical Treatment Decision Act	Arizona Revised Statutes §§ 36-3201, et seq.
Arkansas—Rights of the Terminally Ill Act	Arkansas Ann. Code §§ 20-17-202 et seq.
California—Health Care Decisions Law	California Probate Code §§ 4670 et seq.
Colorado—Medical Treatment Decision Act	Colorado Revised Statutes §§ 15-18-101 et seq.
Connecticut—Removal of Life Support Systems	Connecticut Gen. Statutes §§ 19a-570 et seq.
Delaware—Death With Dignity Act	Delaware Ann. Code Tit. 16 §§ 2501 et seq.
District of Columbia—Natural Death Act	D.C. Ann. Code §§ 7-621 et seq.
Florida—Life Prolonging Procedure Act	Florida Ann. Statutes §§ 765.301 et seq.
Georgia—Living Wills Act	Georgia Ann. Code §§ 31-32-1 et seq.
Hawaii—Medical Treatment Decisions Act	Hawaii Revised Statutes §§ 327E-1 et seq.
Idaho—Natural Death Act	Idaho Ann. Code §§ 39-4501 et seq.
Illinois—Living Will At	Illinois Revised Statutes Ch. 755 §§ 35/1 et seq.
Indiana—Living Wills Act	Indiana Ann. Code §§ 16-36-4-1 et seq.
Iowa—Life Sustaining Procedures Act	Code of Iowa §§ 144A.3 et seq.

STATE STATUTE	CITATION
Kansas—Natural Death Act	Kansas Ann. Statutes §§ 65-28.101 et seq.
Kentucky—Living Will Acct	Kentucky Revised Statutes §§ 311.621 et seq.
Louisiana—Natural Death Act	Louisiana Revised Statutes Tit. 40 §§ 1299.58.1 et seq.
Maine—Living Will Act	Maine Revised Statutes Tit. 18-A, §§ 5-801 et seq.
Maryland—Life Sustaining Procedures Act	Maryland Health General Code Ann. Tit. 5 §§ 5-601 et seq.
Massachusetts	No statutory provision for living will
Michigan	No statutory provision for living will
Minnesota—Adult Health Care Decisions Act	Minnesota Ann. Statutes §§ 145B.01 et seq.
Mississippi—Natural Death Act	Mississippi Ann. Code §§ 41-41-201 et seq.
Missouri—Life Support Declaration	Missouri Ann. Statutes §§ 459.015 et seq.
Montana—Living Will Act	Montana Ann. Code §§ 50-9-101 et seq.
Nebraska—Rights of the Terminally Ill Act	Nebraska Revised Statutes §§ 20-401 et seq.
Nevada—Living Will Statute	Nevada Revised Statutes §§ 449.535 et seq.
New Hampshire—Terminal Care Document	New Hampshire Revised Statutes §§ 137-H:1 et seq.
New Jersey—Living Will Statute	New Jersey Ann. Statutes §§ 26:2H-53 et seq.
New Mexico—Right to Die Act	New Mexico Ann. Statutes §§24-7A-1 et seq.
New York—Public Health Law	New York Public Health Law Art. 29-B; 29-C § 2964 et seq.
North Carolina—Natural Death Act	North Carolina General Statutes §§ 90-320 et seq.
North Dakota—Rights of the Terminally Ill Act	North Dakota Cent. Code §§ 23-06. 4-01 et seq.

STATE STATUTE	CITATION
Ohio—Living Will Statute	Ohio Revised Code §§ 2133.01 et seq.
Oklahoma—Natural Death Act	Oklahoma Ann. Statutes Tit. 63, Ch. 60 §§ 3101.1 et seq.
Oregon—Directive to Physician	Oregon Revised Statutes §§ 127.505 et seq.
Pennsylvania—Advance Directive for Health Care	Pennsylvania Cons. Statutes Tit. 20, §§ 5401 et seq.
Rhode Island—Rights of the Terminally Ill Act	Rhode Island General Laws §§ 23-4.11-1 et seq.
South Carolina—Death with Dignity Act	South Carolina Cent. Code §§ 44-77-10 et seq.
South Dakota—Living Will Statute	South Dakota Ann. Code §§ 34-12D-1 et seq.
Tennessee—Right to Natural Death Act	Tennessee Ann. Code §§ 32-11-101 et seq.
Texas—Advance Directives	Texas Health & Safety Code §§ 166.031 et seq.
Utah—Personal Choice and Living Will Act	Utah Ann. Code §§ 75-2-1101 et seq.
Vermont—Terminal Care Document	Vermont Ann. Statutes. Tit. 18, Ch. 11 §§5251 et seq.
Virginia—Natural Death Act	Virginia Ann. Code §§ 54.1-2981 et seq.
Washington—Natural Death Act	Washington Rev. Code Ann. §§ 70-122.010 et seq.
West Virginia—Natural Death Act	West Virginia Ann. Code Art. 30 §§ 16-30-1 et seq.
Wisconsin—Natural Death Act	Wisconsin Ann. Statutes §§ 154.01 et seq.
Wyoming—Living Will Act	Wyoming Statutes §§ 35-22-101 et seq.

APPENDIX 17:
DURABLE POWER OF ATTORNEY
FOR HEALTH CARE

APPOINTMENT made this_____ day of____, 20___.

I, [insert declarant's name and address], being of sound mind, willfully and voluntarily appoint [insert health care agent's name/address/telephone number], as my Health Care Agent (hereinafter "Agent") with a Durable Power of Attorney to make any and all health care decisions for me, except to the extent stated otherwise in this document.

EFFECTIVE DATE

This Durable Power of Attorney and Appointment of Health Care Agent shall take effect at such time as I become comatose, incapacitated, or otherwise mentally or physically incapable of giving directions or consent regarding the use of life-sustaining procedures or any other health care measures.

"Health care" in this context means any treatment, service, or procedure utilized to maintain, diagnose, or treat any physical or mental condition.

DETERMINATION OF MEDICAL CONDITION

A determination of incapacity shall be certified by my attending physician and by a second physician who is neither employed by the facility where I am a patient nor associated in practice with my attending physician and who shall be appointed to independently assess and evaluate my capacity by the appropriate administrator of the facility where I am a patient.

AUTHORITY OF HEALTH CARE AGENT

My Agent is authorized, in consultation with my attending physician, to direct the withdrawal or withholding of any life-sustaining procedures, as defined herein, as he/she solely in the exercise of his/her judgment shall determine are appropriate to give comply with my wishes and desires.

In addition, my Agent by acceptance of this Appointment agrees and is hereby directed to use his/her best efforts to make those decisions that I would make in the exercise of my right to refuse treatment and not those that he/she or others might believe to be in my best interests.

APPOINTMENT OF ALTERNATE AGENTS

If the person designated as my Agent is unable or unwilling to accept this Appointment, I designate the following persons to serve as my Agent to make health care decisions for me as authorized by this document. They shall serve in the following order:

1. First Alternate Agent: [Name, Address and Telephone No.]

2. Second Alternate Agent: [Name, Address and Telephone No.].

DURATION

[Option 1] I understand that this Power of Attorney exists indefinitely unless I define a shorter time herein or execute a revocation. If I am incapacitated at such time as this Power of Attorney expires (if applicable), the authority I have granted my Agent shall continue until such time as I am capable of giving directions regarding my health care.

[Option 2] This power of attorney ends on the following date: [insert termination date].

COPIES AND DISTRIBUTION

The original of this document is kept at [insert address where original document is kept]. I have made [#] copies of this document. Numbered and signed copies have been provided to the following individuals or institutions: [List names, addresses and phone numbers of individuals and/or institutions holding copies of the document].

Signed in the presence of the witnesses who have signed below this ___ _____day of _____, 20__.

NAME/ADDRESS/SIGNATURE LINE – DECLARANT

STATEMENT OF WITNESSES

I state this____ day of___, 20___, under penalty of perjury, that the Declarant has identified himself/herself to me and that the Declarant signed or acknowledged this Health Care Declaration in my presence.

I believe the Declarant to be of sound mind, and the Declarant has affirmed his/her awareness of the nature of this document and is signing it voluntarily and free from duress. The Declarant requested that I serve as a witness to his/her execution of this document.

I declare that I am not related to the Declarant by blood, marriage, or adoption and that to the best of my knowledge I am not entitled to any part of the estate of the Declarant on the death of the principal under a will or by operation of law.

I am not a provider of health or residential care, an employee of a provider of health or residential care, the operator of a community care facility, or an employee of an operator of a health care facility.

I declare that I have no claim against any portion of the estate of the Declarant upon his/her death, nor any personal financial responsibility for the payment of Declarant's medical bills or any other of Declarant's obligations.

SIGNATURE LINE/ADDRESS/DATE – WITNESS #1

SIGNATURE LINE/ADDRESS/DATE – WITNESS #2

SIGNATURE LINE/ADDRESS/DATE – WITNESS #3

ACCEPTANCE BY HEALTH CARE AGENTS

Health Care Agent (First Choice)

I, [insert name of health care agent], am willing to serve and accept the appointment as the health care agent for [insert name of declarant] as described in this document.

SIGNATURE LINE/ADDRESS/DATE – HEALTH CARE AGENT

Health Care Agent (First Alternate)

I, [insert name of first alternate health care agent], am willing to serve and accept the appointment as the health care agent for [insert name of declarant] as described in this document, if the declarant's first choice cannot serve as health care agent.

SIGNATURE LINE/ADDRESS/DATE – HEALTH CARE AGENT

Health Care Agent (Second Alternate)

I, [insert name of second alternate health care agent], am willing to serve and accept the appointment as the health care agent for [insert name of declarant] as described in this document, if neither the declarant's first choice nor first alternate can serve as health care agent.

SIGNATURE LINE/ADDRESS/DATE – HEALTH CARE AGENT (Second Alternate)

NOTARIAL ACKNOWLEDGMENT

BEFORE ME, the undersigned authority, on this day personally appeared [insert name of declarant], and [names of three witnesses], and [names of three health care agents] known to me to be the declarant, witnesses, and health care agents whose names are subscribed to the foregoing instrument in their respective capacities, and, all of said persons being by me duly sworn, [name of declarant] declared to me and to the said witnesses in my presence that said instrument is (his/her) Durable Power of Attorney for Health Care, and that (he/she) had willingly and voluntarily made and executed it as (his/her) free act and deed for the purposes therein expressed.

SUBSCRIBED AND SWORN TO BEFORE ME by the declarant, [insert name], by the witnesses [insert names], and by the health care agents [insert names] this _____ day of _____, 20_____.

SIGNATURE LINE AND STAMP - NOTARY PUBLIC

APPENDIX 18:
SSA REQUEST TO BE SELECTED
AS REPRESENTATIVE PAYEE
(FORM SSA-11-BK)

SOCIAL SECURITY ADMINISTRATION   **TOE 250**

Form Approved
OMB No. 0960-0014

									FOR SSA USE ONLY
	FOR SSA USE ONLY								
	Name or Bene. Sym.	Program	Date of Birth	Type	Gdn.	Cus.	Inst.	Nam.	
REQUEST TO BE SELECTED AS PAYEE									
									DISTRICT OFFICE CODE
									STATE AND COUNTY CODE:

PRINT IN INK:

The name of the NUMBER HOLDER | SOCIAL SECURITY NUMBER

The name of the PERSON(S) (if different from above) for whom you are filing (the "claimant(s)") | SOCIAL SECURITY NUMBER(S)

Answer item 1 ONLY if you are the claimant and want your benefits paid directly to you.

1. I request that I be paid directly.

   CHECK HERE ☐ and answer only items 3, 5, 6, and 8 before signing the form on page 4.

I REQUEST THAT THE SOCIAL SECURITY, SUPPLEMENTAL SECURITY INCOME, BLACK LUNG OR SPECIAL VETERANS BENEFITS FOR THE CLAIMANT(S) NAMED ABOVE BE PAID TO ME AS REPRESENTATIVE PAYEE.

2. Explain why you think the claimant is not able to handle his/her own benefits.
   (In your answer, describe how he/she manages any money he/she receives now.)

   ☐ Claimant is a minor child.

3. Explain why you would be the best representative payee. (Use Remarks if you need more space.)

4. If you are appointed payee, how will you know about the claimant's needs?

☐ Live with me or in the institution I represent.

☐ Daily visits.

☐ Visits at least once a week.

☐ By other means. Explain:

5. Does the claimant have a court-appointed legal guardian? ☐ YES ☐ NO

IF YES, enter the legal guardian's:

NAME _____

ADDRESS _____

PHONE NUMBER _____

TITLE _____

DATE OF APPOINTMENT _____

Explain the circumstances of the appointment. (Use remarks if you need more space.)

6. (a) Where does the claimant live?

☐ Alone

☐ In my home (Go to (b).)   ☐ In a public institution (Go to (c).)

☐ With a relative (Go to (b).)   ☐ In a private institution (Go to (c).)

☐ With someone else (Go to (b).)   ☐ In a nursing home (Go to (c).)

☐ In a board and care facility (Go to (b).)   ☐ In the institution I represent (Go to (c).)

(b) Enter the names and relationships of any other people who live with the claimant.

NAME	RELATIONSHIP

(c) Enter the claimant's residence and mailing addresses (if different from yours).

Residence: Mailing: Telephone Number:

(d) Do you expect the claimant's living arrangements to change in the next year?

☐ YES ☐ NO   If YES, explain what changes are expected and when they will occur. (Use Remarks if you need more space.)

7. If you are applying on behalf of minor child(ren) and you are not the parent,

Does the child(ren) have a living natural or adoptive parent? ☐ YES ☐ NO

If YES, enter: (a) Name of parent _____

(b) Address of parent _____

(c) Telephone number _____

(d) Does the parent show interest in the child? ☐ YES ☐ NO

Please explain. _____

8. List the names and relationship of any (other) relatives or close friends who have provided support and/or show active interest with the claimant. Describe the type and amount of support and/or how interest is displayed.

NAME	ADDRESS/PHONE NO.	RELATIONSHIP	DESCRIBE SUPPORT/INTEREST

9. Check the block that describes your relationship to the claimant.

(a) ☐ Official of bank, agency or institution with responsibility for the person. Enter below which you represent:

☐ Bank

☐ Social Agency

☐ Public Official

☐ Institution:

☐ Federal

☐ State/Local

☐ Private non-profit

☐ Private proprietary institution. Is the institution licensed under State law? ☐ YES ☐ NO

IF (a) ABOVE CHECKED, COMPLETE ONLY QUESTIONS 10 AND 11 AND SIGN THE FORM ON PAGE 4.

(b) ☐ Parent

(c) ☐ Spouse

(d) ☐ Other Relative - Specify _____

(e) ☐ Legal Representative

(f) ☐ Board and Care Home Operator

(g) ☐ Other Individual - Specify _____

IF (b), (c), (d), or (e) ABOVE CHECKED, GO ON TO QUESTION 12

Form **SSA-11-BK** (03-2006)   EF (03-2006)   Page 2

INFORMATION ABOUT INSTITUTIONS, AGENCIES AND BANKS APPLYING TO BE REPRESENTATIVE PAYEE

10. (a) Enter the name of the institution _____

    (b) Enter the EIN of the institution _____

11. Is the claimant indebted to your institution for past care and maintenance? ☐ YES ☐ NO
If YES, give the amount of the debt, the date(s) the debt was incurred and the description of the debt.

INFORMATION ABOUT INDIVIDUALS APPLYING TO BE REPRESENTATIVE PAYEE

12. Enter: YOUR NAME _____

    DATE OF BIRTH _____

    SOCIAL SECURITY NUMBER _____

    ANY OTHER NAME YOU HAVE USED _____

    OTHER SSN'S YOU HAVE USED _____

13. How long have you known the claimant? _____

14. Does the claimant owe you any money now or will he/she owe you money in the future? ☐ YES ☐ NO
If YES, enter the amount he/she owes you, the date(s) the debt was/will be incurred and describe why the debt was/will be incurred.

15. If the claimant lives with you, who takes care of the claimant when work or other activity takes you away from home? What is his/her relationship to the claimant?

16. (a) Main source of your income

    ☐ Employed (answer (b) below)

    ☐ Self-employed (Type of Business _____)

    ☐ Social Security or Black Lung benefits (Claim Number _____)

    ☐ Pension (describe _____)

    ☐ Supplemental Security Income payments (Claim Number _____)

    ☐ AFDC (County & State _____)

    ☐ Other Welfare (describe _____)

    ☐ Other (describe _____)

    (b) Enter your employer's name and address:

    How long have you been employed by this employer? _____

    (If less than 1 year, enter name and address of previous employer in Remarks.)

17. (a) Have you ever been convicted of a felony? ☐ YES ☐ NO

    If YES: What was the crime? _____

    On what date were you convicted? _____

    What was your sentence? _____

    If imprisoned, when were you released? _____

    If probation was ordered, when did/will your probation end? _____

    (b) Have you ever been convicted of any offense under federal or state law which resulted in imprisonment for more than one year? ☐ YES ☐ NO

    If YES: What was the crime? _____

    On what date were you convicted? _____

    What was your sentence? _____

    If imprisoned, when were you released? _____

    If probation was ordered, when did/will your probation end? _____

Form **SSA-11-BK** (03-2006)   EF (03-2006)   Page 3

18.	Do you have any unsatisfied FELONY warrants (or in jurisdictions that do not define crimes as felonies, a crime punishable by death or imprisonment exceeding 1 year) for your arrest? ☐ YES ☐ NO
	If YES: Date of Warrant_____
	State where warrant was issued_____
19.	How long have you lived at your current address? (Give Date MM/YY) (If less than 1 year, enter previous address in Remarks) _____

REMARKS: *(This space may be used for explaining any answers to the questions. If you need more space, attach a separate sheet.)*

PLEASE READ THE FOLLOWING INFORMATION CAREFULLY BEFORE SIGNING THIS FORM

I/my organization:

- Must use all payments made to me/my organization as the representative payee for the claimant's current needs or (if not currently needed) save them for his/her future needs.
- May be held liable for repayment if I/my organization misuse the payments or if I/my organization am/is at fault for any overpayment of benefits.
- May be punished under Federal law by fine, imprisonment or both if I/my organization am/is found guilty of misuse of Social Security or SSI benefits.

I/my organization will:

- Use the payments for the claimant's current needs and save any currently unneeded benefits for future use.
- File an accounting report on how the payments were used, and make all supporting records available for review if requested by the Social Security Administration.
- Reimburse the amount of any loss suffered by any claimant due to misuse of Social Security or SSI funds by me/my organization.
- Notify the Social Security Administration when the claimant dies, leaves my/my organization's custody or otherwise changes his/her living arrangements or he/she is no longer my/my organization's responsibility.
- Comply with the conditions for reporting certain events (listed on the attached sheets(s) which I/my organization will keep for my/my organization's records) and for returning checks the claimant is not due.
- File an annual report of earnings if required.
- Notify the Social Security Administration as soon as I/my organization can no longer act as representative payee or the claimant no longer needs a payee.

I declare under penalty of perjury that I have examined all the information on this form, and on any accompanying statements or forms, and it is true and correct to the best of my knowledge.

SIGNATURE OF APPLICANT	DATE *(Month, day, year)*
Signature *(First name, middle initial, last name) (Write in ink)*	Telephone number(s) at Which You May Be Contacted During the Day
SIGN HERE ▶	

Print Your Name & Title *(if a representative or employee of an institution/organization)*

Mailing Address *(Number and street, Apt. No., P.O. Box, or Rural Route)*

City and State	Zip Code	Name of County

Residence Address *(Number and street, Apt. No., P.O. Box, or Rural Route)*

City and State	Zip Code	Name of County

Witnesses are only required if this application has been signed by mark (X) above. If signed by mark (X), two witnesses to the signing who know the applicant making the request must sign below, giving their full addresses.

1. SIGNATURE OF WITNESS	2. SIGNATURE OF WITNESS
ADDRESS *(Number and street, City, State and ZIP Code)*	ADDRESS *(Number and street, City, State and ZIP Code)*

Form **SSA-11-BK** (03-2006)   EF (03-2006)   Page 4

SOCIAL SECURITY
Information for Representative Payees Who Receive Social Security Benefits

YOU MUST NOTIFY THE SOCIAL SECURITY ADMINISTRATION PROMPTLY IF ANY OF THE FOLLOWING EVENTS OCCUR AND PROMPTLY RETURN ANY PAYMENT TO WHICH THE CLAIMANT IS NOT ENTITLED:

- the claimant DIES (Social Security entitlement ends the month before the month the claimant dies);
- the claimant MARRIES, if the claimant is entitled to child's, widow's, mother's, father's, widower's or parent's benefits, or to wife's or husband's benefits as a divorced wife/husband, or to special age 72 payments;
- the claimant's marriage ends in DIVORCE or ANNULMENT, if the claimant is entitled to wife's, husband's or special age 72 payments;
- the claimant's SCHOOL ATTENDANCE CHANGES if the claimant is age 18 or over and entitled to child's benefits as a full time student;
- the claimant is entitled as a stepchild and the parents DIVORCE (benefits terminate the month after the month the divorce becomes final);
- the claimant is under FULL RETIREMENT AGE (FRA) and WORKS for more than the annual limit (as determined each year) or more than the allowable time (for work outside the United States);
- the claimant receives a GOVERNMENT PENSION or ANNUITY or the amount of the annuity changes, if the claimant is entitled to husband's, widower's, or divorced spouse's benefits;
- the claimant leaves your custody or care or otherwise CHANGES ADDRESS;
- the claimant NO LONGER HAS A CHILD IN CARE, if he/she is entitled to benefits because of caring for a child under age 16 or who is disabled;
- the claimant is confined to jail, prison, penal institution or correctional facility;
- the claimant is confined to a public institution by court order in connection WITH A CRIME.
- the claimant has an UNSATISFIED FELONY WARRANT (or in jurisdictions that do not define crimes as felonies, a crime punishable by death or imprisonment exceeding 1 year) issued for his/her arrest;
- the claimant is violating a condition of probation or parole under State or Federal law.

IF THE CLAIMANT IS RECEIVING DISABILITY BENEFITS, YOU MUST ALSO REPORT IF:

- the claimant's MEDICAL CONDITION IMPROVES;
- the claimant STARTS WORKING;
- the claimant applies for or receives WORKER'S COMPENSATION BENEFITS, Black Lung Benefits from the Department of Labor, or a public disability benefit;
- the claimant is DISCHARGED FROM THE HOSPITAL (if now hospitalized).

IF THE CLAIMANT IS RECEIVING SPECIAL AGE 72 PAYMENTS, YOU MUST ALSO REPORT IF:

- the claimant or spouse becomes ELIGIBLE FOR PERIODIC GOVERNMENTAL PAYMENTS, whether from the U.S. Federal government or from any State or local government;
- the claimant or spouse receives SUPPLEMENTAL SECURITY INCOME or PUBLIC ASSISTANCE CASH BENEFITS;
- the claimant or spouse MOVES outside the United States (the 50 States, the District of Columbia and the Northern Mariana Islands).

In addition to these events about the claimant, you must also notify us if:

- YOU change your address;
- YOU are convicted of a felony or any offense under State or Federal law which results in imprisonment for more than 1 year;
- YOU have an UNSATISFIED FELONY WARRANT (or in jurisdictions that do not define crimes as felonies, a crime punishable by death or imprisonment exceeding 1 year) issued for your arrest.

BENEFITS MAY STOP IF ANY OF THE ABOVE EVENTS OCCUR. You should read the informational booklet we will send you to see how these events affect benefits. You may make your reports by telephone, mail or in person.

REMEMBER:

- payments must be used for the claimant's current needs or saved if not currently needed;
- you may be held liable for repayment of any payments not used for the claimant's needs or of any over payment that occurred due to your fault;
- you must account for benefits when so asked by the Social Security Administration. You will keep records of how benefits were spent so you can provide us with a correct accounting;
- to tell us as soon as you know you will no longer be able to act as representative payee or the claimant no longer needs a payee.

Keep in mind that benefits may be deposited directly into an account set up for the claimant with you as payee. As soon as you set up such an account, contact us for more information about receiving the claimant's payments using direct deposit.

Form **SSA-11-BK** (03-2006)   EF (03-2006)   Page 5

A REMINDER TO PAYEE APPLICANTS

		SSA OFFICE	DATE REQUEST RECEIVED
TELEPHONE NUMBER(S) TO CALL IF YOU HAVE A QUESTION OR SOMETHING TO REPORT	BEFORE YOU RECEIVE A DECISION NOTICE		
	AFTER YOU RECEIVE A DECISION NOTICE		

RECEIPT FOR YOUR REQUEST

Your request for Social Security benefits on behalf of the individual(s) named below has been received and will be processed as quickly as possible.

You should hear from us within _____ days after you have given us all the information we requested. Some claims may take longer if additional information is needed.

In the meantime, if you change your address, or if there is some other change that may affect the benefits payable,

you — or someone for you — should report the change. The changes to be reported are listed on the reverse.

Always give us the claim number of the beneficiary when writing or telephoning about the claim.

If you have any questions about this application, we will be glad to help you.

BENEFICIARY	SOCIAL SECURITY CLAIM NUMBER

THE PRIVACY ACT

We are required by section 205(j) and 205(a) of the Social Security Act to ask you to give us the information on this form. This information is needed to determine if you are qualified to serve as representative payee. Although responses to these questions are voluntary, you will not be named representative payee unless you give us the answers to these questions.

Sometimes the law requires us to give out the facts on this form without your consent. We must release this information to another person or government agency if Federal law requires that we do so or to do the research and audits needed to administer or improve our representative payee program.

We may also use the information you give us when we match records by computer. Matching programs compare our records with those of other Federal, state or local government agencies. Many agencies may use matching programs to find or prove that a person qualifies for benefits paid by the Federal government. The law allows us to do this even if you do not agree to it.

Explanation about these and other reasons why information you provide us may be used or given out are available in Social Security offices. If you want to learn more about this, contact any Social Security office.

Paperwork Reduction Act Statement - This information collection meets the requirements of 44 U.S.C. § 3507, as amended by section 2 of the Paperwork Reduction Act of 1995. You do not need to answer these questions unless we display a valid Office of Management and Budget control number. We estimate that it will take about 10.5 minutes to read the instructions, gather the facts, and answer the questions. **SEND OR BRING THE COMPLETED FORM TO YOUR LOCAL SOCIAL SECURITY OFFICE. The office is listed under U. S. Government agencies in your telephone directory or you may call Social Security at 1-800-772-1213.** *You may send comments on our time estimate above to: SSA, 6401 Security Blvd., Baltimore, MD 21235-6401.* **Send *only* comments relating to our time estimate to this address, not the completed form.**

Form **SSA-11-BK** (03-2006)   EF (03-2006)   Page 6

SUPPLEMENTAL SECURITY INCOME
Information for Representative Payees Who Receive Social Security Benefits

YOU MUST NOTIFY THE SOCIAL SECURITY ADMINISTRATION PROMPTLY IF ANY OF THE FOLLOWING EVENTS OCCUR AND PROMPTLY RETURN ANY PAYMENT TO WHICH THE CLAIMANT IS NOT ENTITLED:

- the claimant or any member of the claimant's household DIES (SSI eligibility ends with the month in which the claimant dies);
- the claimant's HOUSEHOLD CHANGES (someone moves in/out of the place where the claimant lives);
- the claimant LEAVES THE U.S. (the 50 states, the District of Columbia, and the Northern Mariana Islands) for 30 consecutive days or more;
- the claimant MOVES or otherwise changes the place where he/she actually lives (including adoption, and whereabouts unknown);
- the claimant is ADMITTED TO A HOSPITAL, skilled nursing facility, nursing home, intermediate care facility, or other institution;
- the INCOME of the claimant or anyone in the claimant's household CHANGES (this includes income paid by an organization or employer, as well as monetary benefits from other sources);
- the RESOURCES of the claimant or anyone in the claimant's household CHANGES (this includes when conserved funds reach over $2,000);
- the claimant or anyone in the claimant's household MARRIES;
- the marriage of the claimant or anyone in the claimant's household ends in DIVORCE or ANNULMENT;
- the claimant SEPARATES from his/her spouse;
- the claimant is confined to jail, prison, penal institution or correctional facility;
- the claimant is confined to a public institution by court order in connection WITH A CRIME;
- the claimant has an UNSATISFIED FELONY WARRANT (or in jurisdictions that do not define crimes as felonies, a crime punishable by death or imprisonment exceeding 1 year) issued for his/her arrest;
- the claimant is violating a condition of probation or parole under State or Federal law.

IF THE CLAIMANT IS RECEIVING PAYMENTS DUE TO DISABILITY OR BLINDNESS, YOU MUST ALSO REPORT IF:
- the claimant's MEDICAL CONDITION IMPROVES;
- the claimant GOES TO WORK;
- the claimant's VISION IMPROVES, if the claimant is entitled due to blindness;

In addition to these events about the claimant, you must also notify us if:
- YOU change your address;
- YOU are convicted of a felony or any offense under State or Federal law which results in imprisonment for more than 1 year;
- YOU have an UNSATISFIED FELONY WARRANT (or in jurisdictions that do not define crimes as felonies, a crime punishable by death or imprisonment exceeding 1 year) issued for your arrest.

PAYMENT MAY STOP IF ANY OF THE ABOVE EVENTS OCCUR. You should read the informational booklet we will send you to see how these events affect benefits. You may make your reports by telephone, mail or in person.

REMEMBER:
- payments must be used for the claimant's current needs or saved if not currently needed. (Savings are considered resources and may affect the claimant's eligibility to payment.)
- you may be held liable for repayment of any payments not used for the claimant's needs or of any overpayment that occurred due to your fault;
- you must account for benefits when so asked by the Social Security Administration. You will keep records of how benefits were spent so you can provide us with a correct accounting;
- to let us know as soon as you know you are unable to continue as representative payee or the claimant no longer needs a payee;
- you will be asked to help in periodically redetermining the claimant's continued eligibility or payment. You will need to keep evidence to help us with the redetermination (e.g., evidence of income and living arrangements).
- you may be required to obtain medical treatment for the claimant's disabling condition if he/she is eligible under the childhood disability provision.

Keep in mind that payments may be deposited directly into an account set up for the claimant with you as payee. As soon as you set up such an account, contact us for more information about receiving the claimant's payments using direct deposit.

Form **SSA-11-BK** (03-2006)   EF (03-2006)   Page 7

A REMINDER TO PAYEE APPLICANTS

TELEPHONE NUMBER(S) TO CALL IF YOU HAVE A QUESTION OR SOMETHING TO REPORT	BEFORE YOU RECEIVE A DECISION NOTICE	SSA OFFICE	DATE REQUEST RECEIVED
	AFTER YOU RECEIVE A DECISION NOTICE		

RECEIPT FOR YOUR REQUEST

Your request for SSI payments on behalf of the individual(s) named below has been received and will be processed as quickly as possible.

You should hear from us within _____ days after you have given us all the information we requested. Some claims may take longer if additional information is needed.

In the meantime, if you change your address, or if there is some other change that may affect the benefits payable,

you — or someone for you — should report the change. The changes to be reported are listed on the reverse.

Always give us the claim number of the beneficiary when writing or telephoning about the claim.

If you have any questions about this application, we will be glad to help you.

BENEFICIARY	SOCIAL SECURITY CLAIM NUMBER

THE PRIVACY ACT

We are required by section 205(j) and 205(a) of the Social Security Act to ask you to give us the information on this form. This information is needed to determine if you are qualified to serve as representative payee. Although responses to these questions are voluntary, you will not be named representative payee unless you give us the answers to these questions.

Sometimes the law requires us to give out the facts on this form without your consent. We must release this information to another person or government agency if Federal law requires that we do so or to do the research and audits needed to administer or improve our representative payee program.

We may also use the information you give us when we match records by computer. Matching programs compare our records with those of other Federal, state or local government agencies. Many agencies may use matching programs to find or prove that a person qualifies for benefits paid by the Federal government. The law allows us to do this even if you do not agree to it.

Explanation about these and other reasons why information you provide us may be used or given out are available in Social Security offices. If you want to learn more about this, contact any Social Security office.

Paperwork Reduction Act Statement - This information collection meets the requirements of 44 U.S.C. § 3507, as amended by section 2 of the Paperwork Reduction Act of 1995. You do not need to answer these questions unless we display a valid Office of Management and Budget control number. We estimate that it will take about 10.5 minutes to read the instructions, gather the facts, and answer the questions. **SEND OR BRING THE COMPLETED FORM TO YOUR LOCAL SOCIAL SECURITY OFFICE. The office is listed under U. S. Government agencies in your telephone directory or you may call Social Security at 1-800-772-1213.** *You may send comments on our time estimate above to: SSA, 6401 Security Blvd., Baltimore, MD 21235-6401. Send only comments relating to our time estimate to this address, not the completed form.*

Form **SSA-11-BK** (03-2006)   EF (03-2006)   Page 8

BLACK LUNG BENEFITS
Information for Representative Payees Who Receive Black Lung Benefits

YOU MUST NOTIFY THE SOCIAL SECURITY ADMINISTRATION PROMPTLY IF ANY OF THE FOLLOWING EVENTS OCCUR AND PROMPTLY RETURN ANY PAYMENT TO WHICH THE CLAIMANT IS NOT ENTITLED:

- the claimant DIES;
- the claimant receives STATE WORKER'S COMPENSATION based on the miner's disability, or the amount of such compensation changes;
- the miner receives UNEMPLOYMENT INSURANCE;
- the claimant IS WORKING or RETURNS TO WORK;
- the claimant MARRIES or REMARRIES, if the claimant is entitled to child's, widow's, brother's or sister's benefits;
- the claimant begins to RECEIVE SUPPORT PAYMENTS from his/her spouse, if the claimant is entitled to brother's or sister's benefits;
- the claimant is ADOPTED, if the claimant is entitled to child's benefits;
- the claimant's MEDICAL CONDITION IMPROVES, if the claimant is entitled to disabled child's brother's or sister's benefits;
- the claimant is age 18 to 23 and STOPS ATTENDING SCHOOL, if the claimant is receiving child's, sister's or brother's benefits.

In addition to these events about the claimant, you must also notify us if:
- YOU change your address;
- YOU are convicted of a felony or any offer under State or Federal law which results in imprisonment for more than 1 year;
- YOU have an UNSATISFIED FELONY WARRANT (or in jurisdictions that do not define crimes as felonies, a crime punishable by death or imprisonment exceeding 1 year) issued for your arrest.

BENEFITS MAY STOP IF ANY OF THE ABOVE EVENTS OCCUR. You should read the informational booklet we will send you to see how these events affect benefits. You may make your reports by telephone, mail or in person.

REMEMBER:
- payments must be used for the claimant's current needs or saved if not currently needed;
- you may be held liable for repayment of any payments not used for the claimant's needs or of any overpayment that occurred due to your fault;
- you must account for benefits when so asked by the Social Security Administration. You will keep records of how benefits were spent so you can provide us with a correct accounting;
- to let us know as soon as you know you are unable to continue as representative payee or the claimant no longer needs a payee.

Keep in mind that benefits may be deposited directly into an account set up for the claimant with you as payee. As soon as you set up such an account, contact us for more information about receiving the claimant's payments using direct deposit.

A REMINDER TO PAYEE APPLICANTS

TELEPHONE NUMBER(S) TO CALL IF YOU HAVE A QUESTION OR SOMETHING TO REPORT	BEFORE YOU RECEIVE A DECISION NOTICE	SSA OFFICE	DATE REQUEST RECEIVED
	AFTER YOU RECEIVE A DECISION NOTICE		

RECEIPT FOR YOUR REQUEST

Your request for Black Lung benefits on behalf of the individual(s) named below has been received and will be processed as quickly as possible.

You should hear from us within _____ days after you have given us all the information we requested. Some claims may take longer if additional information is needed.

In the meantime, if you change your address, or if there is some other change that may affect the benefits payable,

you — or someone for you — should report the change. The changes to be reported are listed on the reverse.

Always give us the claim number of the beneficiary when writing or telephoning about the claim.

If you have any questions about this application, we will be glad to help you.

BENEFICIARY	SOCIAL SECURITY CLAIM NUMBER

THE PRIVACY ACT

We are required by section 205(j) and 205(a) of the Social Security Act to ask you to give us the information on this form. This information is needed to determine if you are qualified to serve as representative payee. Although responses to these questions are voluntary, you will not be named representative payee unless you give us the answers to these questions.

Sometimes the law requires us to give out the facts on this form without your consent. We must release this information to another person or government agency if Federal law requires that we do so or to do the research and audits needed to administer or improve our representative payee program.

We may also use the information you give us when we match records by computer. Matching programs compare our records with those of other Federal, state or local government agencies. Many agencies may use matching programs to find or prove that a person qualifies for benefits paid by the Federal government. The law allows us to do this even if you do not agree to it.

Explanation about these and other reasons why information you provide us may be used or given out are available in Social Security offices. If you want to learn more about this, contact any Social Security office.

Paperwork Reduction Act Statement - This information collection meets the requirements of 44 U.S.C. § 3507, as amended by section 2 of the Paperwork Reduction Act of 1995. You do not need to answer these questions unless we display a valid Office of Management and Budget control number. We estimate that it will take about 10.5 minutes to read the instructions, gather the facts, and answer the questions. **SEND OR BRING THE COMPLETED FORM TO YOUR LOCAL SOCIAL SECURITY OFFICE. The office is listed under U. S. Government agencies in your telephone directory or you may call Social Security at 1-800-772-1213.** *You may send comments on our time estimate above to: SSA, 6401 Security Blvd., Baltimore, MD 21235-6401. Send only comments relating to our time estimate to this address, not the completed form.*

Form **SSA-11-BK** (03-2006)   EF (03-2006)   Page 10

Guardianship, Conservatorship and the Law   **147**

SPECIAL BENEFITS FOR WORLD WAR II VETERANS
Information for Representative Payees Who Receive Special Benefits for WW II Veterans

YOU MUST NOTIFY THE SOCIAL SECURITY ADMINISTRATION PROMPTLY IF ANY OF THE FOLLOWING EVENTS OCCUR AND PROMPTLY RETURN ANY PAYMENT TO WHICH THE CLAIMANT IS NOT ENTITLED:

- the claimant DIES (special veterans entitlement ends the month after the claimant dies);
- the claimant returns to the United States for a calendar month or longer;
- the claimant moves or changes the place where he/she actually lives;
- the claimant receives a pension, annuity or other recurring payment (includes workers' compensation, veterans benefits or disability benefits), or the amount of the annuity changes;
- the claimant is or has been deported or removed from U.S.;
- the claimant has an UNSATISFIED FELONY WARRANT (or in jurisdictions that do not define crimes as felonies, a crime punishable by death or imprisonment exceeding 1 year) issued for his/her arrest;
- the claimant is violating a condition of probation or parole under State or Federal law.

In addition to these events about the claimant, you must also notify us if:
- YOU change your address;
- YOU are convicted of a felony or any offense under State or Federal law which results in imprisonment for more than 1 year;
- YOU have an UNSATISFIED FELONY WARRANT (or in jurisdictions that do not define crimes as felonies, a crime punishable by death or imprisonment exceeding 1 year) issued for your arrest.

BENEFITS MAY STOP IF ANY OF THE ABOVE EVENTS OCCUR. You can make your reports by telephone, mail or in person. You can contact any U.S. Embassy, Consulate, Veterans Affairs Regional Office in the Philippines or any U.S. Social Security Office.

REMEMBER:
- payments must be used for the claimant's current needs or saved if not currently needed;
- you may be held liable for repayment of any payments not used for the claimant's needs or of any overpayment that occurred due to your fault;
- you must account for benefits when so asked by the Social Security Administration. You will keep records of how benefits were spent so you can provide us with a correct accounting;
- to let us know, as soon as you know you are unable to continue as representative payee or the claimant no longer needs a payee.

Form **SSA-11-BK** (03-2006)   EF (03-2006)   Page 11

A REMINDER TO PAYEE APPLICANTS

TELEPHONE NUMBER(S) TO CALL IF YOU HAVE A QUESTION OR SOMETHING TO REPORT	BEFORE YOU RECEIVE A DECISION NOTICE	SSA OFFICE	DATE REQUEST RECEIVED
	AFTER YOU RECEIVE A DECISION NOTICE		

RECEIPT FOR YOUR REQUEST

Your request for Special benefits for WW II Veterans on behalf of the individual(s) named below has been received and will be processed as quickly as possible.

You should hear from us within _____ days after you have given us all the information we requested. Some claims may take longer if additional information is needed.

In the meantime, if you change your address, or if there is some other change that may affect the benefits payable,

you — or someone for you — should report the change. The changes to be reported are listed on the reverse.

Always give us the claim number of the beneficiary when writing or telephoning about the claim.

If you have any questions about this application, we will be glad to help you.

BENEFICIARY	SOCIAL SECURITY CLAIM NUMBER

THE PRIVACY ACT

We are required by section 205(j) and 205(a) of the Social Security Act to ask you to give us the information on this form. This information is needed to determine if you are qualified to serve as representative payee. Although responses to these questions are voluntary, you will not be named representative payee unless you give us the answers to these questions.

Sometimes the law requires us to give out the facts on this form without your consent. We must release this information to another person or government agency if Federal law requires that we do so or to do the research and audits needed to administer or improve our representative payee program.

We may also use the information you give us when we match records by computer. Matching programs compare our records with those of other Federal, state or local government agencies. Many agencies may use matching programs to find or prove that a person qualifies for benefits paid by the Federal government. The law allows us to do this even if you do not agree to it.

Explanation about these and other reasons why information you provide us may be used or given out are available in Social Security offices. If you want to learn more about this, contact any Social Security office.

Paperwork Reduction Act Statement - This information collection meets the requirements of 44 U.S.C. § 3507, as amended by section 2 of the Paperwork Reduction Act of 1995. You do not need to answer these questions unless we display a valid Office of Management and Budget control number. We estimate that it will take about 10.5 minutes to read the instructions, gather the facts, and answer the questions. **SEND OR BRING THE COMPLETED FORM TO YOUR LOCAL SOCIAL SECURITY OFFICE. The office is listed under U. S. Government agencies in your telephone directory or you may call Social Security at 1-800-772-1213.** *You may send comments on our time estimate above to: SSA, 6401 Security Blvd., Baltimore, MD 21235-6401. Send only comments relating to our time estimate to this address, not the completed form.*

Form **SSA-11-BK** (03-2006)   EF (03-2006)   Page 12

GLOSSARY

Accrue—To occur or come into existence.

Acknowledgement—A formal declaration of one's signature before a notary public.

Act—Legislation passed by Congress.

Action at Law—A judicial proceeding whereby one party prosecutes another for a wrong done.

Actionable—Giving rise to a cause of action.

Actionable Negligence—The breach or nonperformance of a legal duty through neglect or carelessness, resulting in damage or injury to another.

Active Euthanasia—The inducement of gentle death solely by means without which life would continue naturally.

Activities of Daily Living—Activities usually performed during the course of a normal day, e.g., bathing, dressing, eating, etc.

Actual Damages—Actual damages are those damages directly referable to the breach or tortious act, and which can be readily proven to have been sustained, and for which the injured party should be compensated as a matter of right.

Ad Damnum Clause—The clause in a complaint that sets forth the amount of damages demanded.

Adult Protective Services—Agency that investigates and resolves reports of alleged psychological and physical abuse, neglect, self-neglect, or financial exploitation of vulnerable adults.

Advance Directive—A written document that expresses an individual's preferences and instructions regarding health care in the event the individual becomes incompetent or unable to communicate or loses decision-making abilities.

Adjudication—The determination of a controversy and pronouncement of judgment.

Admissible Evidence—Evidence that may be received by a trial court to assist the trier of fact, either the judge or jury, in deciding a dispute.

Admitting Physician—The doctor that admits a person to a hospital or other in-patient health facility.

Adversary—Opponent or litigant in a legal controversy or litigation.

Adversary Proceeding—A proceeding involving a real controversy contested by two opposing parties.

Affidavit—A sworn or affirmed statement made in writing and signed; if sworn, it is notarized.

Affirmative Defense—In a pleading, a matter constituting a defense.

Agency—The relationship between a principal and an agent who is employed by the principal, to perform certain acts dealing with third parties.

Agent—An individual designated in a power of attorney for health care to make a health-care decision for the individual granting the power.

Allegation—Statement of the issue that the contributing party is prepared to prove.

Allocation—The system of ensuring that organs and tissues are distributed fairly to patients who are in need.

Alzheimer's Disease—Disorder involving deterioration of mental functions resulting from changes in brain tissues.

Ambulatory Care—Health services that do not require in-patient hospital care.

Amend—As in a pleading, to make an addition to, or a subtraction from, an already existing pleading.

American Bar Association (ABA)—A national organization of lawyers and law students.

American Arbitration Association (AAA)—National organization of arbitrators from whose panel arbitrators are selected for labor and civil disputes.

American Civil Liberties Union (ACLU)—A nationwide organization dedicated to the enforcement and preservation of rights and civil liberties guaranteed by the federal and state constitutions.

Anatomical Donation—The act of giving one's organs or tissue to someone else.

Answer—In a civil proceeding, the principal pleading on the part of the defendant in response to the plaintiff's complaint.

Appeal—Resort to a higher court for the purpose of obtaining a review of a lower court decision.

Appearance—To come into court, personally or through an attorney, after being summoned.

Appellate Court—A court having jurisdiction to review the law as applied to a prior determination of the same case.

Arbitration—The reference of a dispute to an impartial person chosen by the parties to the dispute who agree in advance to abide by the arbitrator's award issued after a hearing at which both parties have an opportunity to be heard.

Arbitration Acts—Federal and state laws that provide for submission of disputes to the process of arbitration.

Arbitration Board—A panel of arbitrators appointed to hear and decide a dispute according to the rules of arbitration.

Arbitration Clause—A clause inserted in a contract providing for compulsory arbitration in case of a dispute as to the rights or liabilities under such contract.

Arbitrator—A private, disinterested person, chosen by the parties to a disputed question, for the purpose of hearing their contention, and awarding judgment to the prevailing party.

Argument—A discourse set forth for the purpose of establishing one's position in a controversy.

Artificial Nutrition and Hydration – Food, water or other fluids that are artificially administered.

Assault—A willful attempt or threat to harm another person, which causes apprehension in that person.

Assessment—The gathering of information in order to evaluate a person's health and health-care needs.

Assumption of Risk—The legal doctrine that a plaintiff may not recover for an injury to which he assents.

Attending Physician—The doctor who is the primary caregiver for a particular patient.

Attestation—The act of witnessing an instrument in writing at the request of the party making the same, and subscribing it as a witness.

Attorney Ad Litem—A lawyer appointed by the court to represent the proposed ward during the guardianship proceedings and advocate for the proposed ward's wishes and desires.

Attorney-In-Fact—An attorney-in-fact is an agent or representative of another given authority to act in that person's name and place pursuant to a document called a "power of attorney."

Best Interest—In the context of refusal of medical treatment or end-of-life court opinions, a standard for making health care decisions based on what others believe to be "best" for a patient by weighing the benefits and the burdens of continuing, withholding or withdrawing treatment.

Battery—The unlawful application of force to the person of another.

Bedsore—A pressure-induced skin ulceration.

Bench—The court and the judges composing the court collectively.

Beneficiary—A person who is designated to receive property upon the death of another, such as the beneficiary of a life insurance policy, who receives the proceeds upon the death of the insured.

Benefits and Burdens—A commonly used guideline for deciding whether or not to withhold or withdraw medical treatments.

Bequest—Refers to a gift of personal property contained in a will.

Best Evidence Rule—The rule of law that requires the original of a writing, recording or photograph to be produced in order to prove its authenticity.

Best Interest—In the context of refusal of medical treatment or end-of-life court opinions, a standard for making health care decisions based on what others believe to be "best" for a patient by weighing the benefits and the burdens of continuing, withholding or withdrawing treatment.

Bill of Particulars—A request by a party for an amplification of the pleading to which it relates.

Bill of Rights—The first eight amendments to the United States Constitution.

Bond—An insurance policy required by the Court in an amount set by the judge to cover the assets of the estate.

Brain Death—Occurs when a person's brain activity stops permanently after which it is impossible to return to life.

Breach of Contract—The failure, without any legal excuse, to perform any promise that forms the whole or the part of a contract.

Breach of Duty—In a general sense, any violation or omission of a legal or moral duty.

Burden of Proof—The duty of a party to substantiate an allegation or issue to convince the trier of fact as to the truth of their claim.

Burial Trust Fund—An account established for burial purposes, usually held by a bank.

Capacity—Capacity is the legal qualification concerning the ability of one to understand the nature and effects of one's acts. In relation to end-of-life decision-making, a patient has medical decision making capacity if he or she has the ability to understand the medical problem and the risks and benefits of the available treatment options.

Caption—The heading of a legal document which contains the name of the court, the index number assigned to the matter, and the names of the parties.

Cardiopulmonary Resuscitation—Cardiopulmonary resuscitation (CPR) is a group of treatments used when someone's heart and/or breathing stops in an attempt to restart the heart and breathing, including mouth-to-mouth breathing, pressing on the chest to mimic the heart's function and cause blood to circulate, electric shock, and heart-stimulating drugs.

Cause of Action—The factual basis for bringing a lawsuit.

Child Abuse—Any form of cruelty to a child's physical, moral or mental well-being.

Child Protective Agency—A state agency responsible for the investigation of child abuse and neglect reports.

Child Welfare—A generic term that embraces the totality of measures necessary for a child's well being; physical, moral and mental.

Circumstantial Evidence—Indirect evidence by which a principal fact may be inferred.

Civil Action—An action maintained to protect a private, civil right as opposed to a criminal action.

Civil Court—The court designed to resolve disputes arising under the common law and civil statutes.

Civil Law—Law that applies to non-criminal actions.

Clear and Convincing Evidence—A high measure or degree of proof that may be required legally to prove a patient's wishes.

Codicil—A document modifying an existing will which, in order to be valid, must be formally drafted and witnessed according to statutory requirements.

Coerce—To compel by pressure, threat, or force.

Compensatory Damages—Compensatory damages are those damages directly referable to a breach or tortious act, and which can be readily proven to have been sustained, and for which the injured party should be compensated as a matter of right.

Competent Adult—An adult who is alert, capable of understanding a lay description of medical procedures and able to appreciate the consequences of providing, withholding, or withdrawing medical procedures.

Complaint—In a civil proceeding, the first pleading of the plaintiff setting out the facts on which the claim for relief is based.

Compromise and Settlement—An arrangement arrived at, either in court or out of court, for settling a dispute upon what appears to the parties to be equitable terms.

Compulsory Arbitration—Arbitration that occurs when the consent of one of the parties is enforced by statutory provisions.

Conclusion of Fact—A conclusion reached by natural inference and based solely on the facts presented.

Conclusion of Law—A conclusion reached through the application of rules of law.

Conclusive Evidence—Evidence that is incontrovertible.

Conservatee—An incompetent or incapacitated person placed under the care of a conservator by the court.

Conservator—An individual, agency, or corporation appointed by the court to manage the financial resources of a disabled person.

Conservatorship—A legal relationship between a conservator and a conservatee.

Constitution—The fundamental principles of law, which frame a governmental system.

Constitutional Right—Refers to the individual liberties granted by the constitution of a state or the federal government.

Contingency Fee—The fee charged by an attorney, which is dependent upon a successful outcome in the case, and is often agreed to be a percentage of the party's recovery.

Contribution—Sharing of a loss or payment among two or more parties.

Contributory Negligence—The act or omission amounting to want of ordinary care on the part of the complaining party which, concurring with the defendant's negligence, is the proximate cause of his or her injury.

Co-payment—The amount the insured may have to pay each time they receive services under their health plan

Coroner—The public official whose responsibility it is to investigate the circumstances and causes of deaths that occur within his or her jurisdiction.

Costs—A sum payable by the losing party to the successful party for his or her expenses in prosecuting or defending a case.

Counterclaims—Counterdemands made by a respondent in his or her favor against a claimant. They are not mere answers or denials of the claimant's allegation.

Court—The branch of government responsible for the resolution of disputes arising under the laws of the government.

Cross-claim—Claim litigated by co-defendants or co- plaintiffs, against each other, and not against a party on the opposing side of the litigation.

Cross-Examination—The questioning of a witness by someone other than the one who called the witness to the stand concerning matters about which the witness testified during direct examination.

Custodial Care—Nonskilled, personal care, such as assistance with activities of daily living.

Damages—In general, damages refers to monetary compensation which the law awards to one who has been injured by the actions of another, such as in the case of tortious conduct or breach of contractual obligations.

Decedent—A deceased person.

Decree—A decision or order of the court.

Defendant—In a civil proceeding, the party responding to the complaint.

Defense—Opposition to the truth or validity of the plaintiff's claims.

Dehydration—Condition whereby a person's loss of bodily fluid exceeds his or her fluid intake.

Delirium—A mix of short-term problems with focusing or shifting attention, being confused and not being aware of one's surroundings.

Dementia—The irreversible deterioration of mental faculties.

Deposition—A method of pretrial discovery that consists of a statement of a witness under oath, taken in question and answer form as it would be in court, with opportunity given to the adversary to be present and cross-examine.

Discharge Plan—A plan that describes the arrangements for any health care services a patient may need after leaving the hospital.

Discovery—Modern pretrial procedure by which one party gains information held by another party.

Do-Not-Resuscitate (DNR) Order—A DNR order is a physician's written order instructing health care providers not to attempt cardiopulmonary resuscitation (CPR) in case of cardiac or respiratory arrest.

Due Process Rights—All rights, which are of such fundamental importance as to require compliance with due process standards of fairness and justice.

Durable Power of Attorney for Health Care—Also known as a "health care proxy," refers to a document naming a person to make medical decisions in the event that the individual becomes unable to make those decisions on his or her own behalf.

Duress—Refers to the action of one person which compels another to do something he or she would not otherwise do.

Duty—The obligation, to which the law will give recognition and effect, to conform to a particular standard of conduct toward another.

Edema—Excessive accumulation of water in the tissues.

Elder Law—Laws regarding the rights of elderly people.

Elopement—The ability of a nursing home resident, who is not capable of self-preservation, to successfully leave the nursing home unsupervised and undetected and enter into a harmful situation.

Emergency Medical Services (EMS)—A group of governmental and private agencies that employ paramedics, first responders, and other ambulance crew to provide emergency care to persons outside of health care facilities.

End-Stage Organ Disease—A disease that ultimately leads to functional failure of an organ, e.g., emphysema (lungs), cardiomyopathy (heart), and polycystic kidney disease (kidneys).

End-Stage Renal Disease (ESRD)—A very serious and life-threatening kidney disease, which is treated by dialysis and kidney transplantation.

Estate—Both real and personal, tangible and intangible, and includes anything that may be the subject of ownership.

Euthanasia—The act of painlessly assisting in the death of a person suffering from terminal illness or other prolonged suffering. Literally means "good death" in Greek.

Execution—The performance of all acts necessary to render a written instrument complete, such as signing, sealing, acknowledging, and delivering the instrument.

Expert Witness—A witness who has special knowledge about a certain subject, upon which he or she will testify, which knowledge is not normally possessed by the average person.

Eyewitness—A person who can testify about a matter because of his or her own presence at the time of the event.

Fact Finder—In a judicial or administrative proceeding, the person, or group of persons, that has the responsibility of determining the acts relevant to decide a controversy.

Fiduciary—A person or entity to whom property management or other responsibility is entrusted.

Finding—Decisions made by the court on issues of fact or law.

Foreseeability—A concept used to limit the liability of a party for the consequences of his acts to consequences that are within the scope of a foreseeable risk.

Fraud—A false representation of a matter of fact, whether by words or by conduct, by false or misleading allegations, or by concealment of that which should have been disclosed, which deceives and is intended to deceive another, and thereby causes injury to that person.

General Damages—General damages are those damages directly referable to the breach or tortious act and which can be readily proven to have been sustained, and for which the injured party should be compensated as a matter of right.

Gerontology—The study of the elderly and the aging process.

Gross Negligence—The intentional failure to meet the required standard of care in reckless disregard of the consequences to another.

Guardian—A person who is entrusted with the management of the property and/or person of another who is incapable, due to age or incapacity, to administer their own affairs.

Guardian Ad Litem—A disinterested person who is appointed by the court on behalf of the ward to represent the ward's best interest.

Guardian of the Estate—A guardian who possesses any or all powers and rights with regard to the property of the ward.

Guardian of the Person—A person who is responsible for and who advocates for the health, well-being and personal needs of the ward.

Guardian of the Person and Estate—A person who acts in both capacities for a ward.

Health Care—Any care, treatment, service, or procedure to maintain, diagnose, or otherwise affect an individual's physical or mental condition.

Health Care Agent—The person named in an advance directive or as permitted under state law to make health care decisions on behalf of a person who is no longer able to make medical decisions.

Health Care Decision—A decision made by an individual or the individual's agent, guardian, or surrogate, regarding the individual's health care, including: (1) selection and discharge of health-care providers and institutions; (2) approval or disapproval of diagnostic tests, surgical procedures, programs of medication, and orders not to resuscitate; and (3) directions to provide, withhold, or withdraw artificial nutrition and hydration and all other forms of health care.

Health Care Institution—An institution, facility, or agency licensed, certified, or otherwise authorized or permitted by law to provide health care in the ordinary course of business.

Health Care Provider—A person who is licensed, certified, registered, or otherwise authorized by law to administer or provide health care in the ordinary course of business or in the practice of a profession.

Health Care Proxy—Any person lawfully designated to act on behalf of an individual.

Hospice Care—A program model for delivering palliative care to individuals who are in the final stages of terminal illness.

Illegal—Against the law.

Immaterial—Evidence that is not offered to prove a material issue.

Impeach—A showing by means of evidence that the testimony of a witness was unworthy of belief. Also refers to the process of charging a public official with a wrong while still holding office.

Impleader—The process of bringing a third potentially liable party into a pending suit.

Implied Consent—Consent that is manifested by signs, actions or facts, or by inaction or silence, which raises a presumption that consent has been given.

Incapacitated Person—An adult who, because of a physical or mental condition, is substantially unable to feed, clothe or shelter him or herself, to care for his or her physical health, or to manage his or her financial affairs.

Incapacity—Incapacity is a defense to breach of contract that refers to a lack of legal, physical or intellectual power to enter into a contract.

Incompetency—Lack of legal qualification or fitness to discharge a legally required duty or to handle one's own affairs; also refers to matters not admissible in evidence.

Infancy—The state of a person who is under the age of legal majority.

Informed Consent—The requirement that a patient be apprised of the nature and risks of a medical procedure before the physician can validly claim exemption from liability for battery, or from responsibility for medical complications.

Injury—Any damage done to another's person, rights, reputation or property.

Inspection Report—Written findings that support a federal or state determination that a nursing home failed to meet certain federal regulations or state requirements.

Intentional Tort—A tort or wrong perpetrated by one who intends to do that which the law has declared wrong, as contrasted with negligence in which the tortfeasor fails to exercise that degree of care in doing what is otherwise permissible.

Interested Parties—Heirs, devises, children, spouses, creditors, beneficiaries and any others having a right in, or claims against, the estate of a ward or protected person that may be affected by guardianship proceedings.

Interrogatories—A pretrial discovery method whereby written questions are served by one party to the action upon the other, who must reply, in writing, under oath.

Intubation—Refers to "endotracheal intubation"—i.e., the insertion of a tube through the mouth or nose into the trachea to create and maintain an open airway to assist breathing.

Joint and Several—The rights and liabilities shared among a group of people individually and collectively.

Judge—The individual who presides over a court, and whose function it is to determine controversies.

Judgment—A judgment is a final determination by a court of law concerning the rights of the parties to a lawsuit.

Jurisdiction—The power to hear and determine a case.

Jury—A group of individuals summoned to decide the facts in issue in a lawsuit.

Jury Trial—A trial during which the evidence is presented to a jury so that they can determine the issues of fact, and render a verdict based upon the law as it applies to their findings of fact.

Lay Witness—Any witness not testifying as an expert witness.

Legal Aid—A national organization established to provide legal services to those who are unable to afford private representation.

Legal Capacity—Referring to the legal capacity to sue, it is the requirement that a person bringing the lawsuit have a sound mind, be of lawful age, and be under no restraint or legal disability.

Legal Representative—Refers to a representative payee, a guardian or conservator acting for a ward or conservatee, a trustee or custodian of a trust or custodianship of which the ward or conservatee is a beneficiary, or an agent designated under a power of attorney, whether for health care or property, in which the ward or conservatee is identified as the principal.

Legislation—Laws enacted by state or federal representatives.

Letters—Refers to letters of conservatorship and/or letters of guardianship.

Letter of Conservatorship—An official letter that serves as written evidence of the appointment of a conservator and the authority of the conservator to act for the conservatee.

Letter of Guardianship—An official letter that serves as written evidence of the appointment of a guardian and the authority of the guardian to act for the ward.

Life Expectancy—The period of time that a person is statistically expected to live, based on such factors as their present age and sex.

Life Insurance—A contract between an insured and an insurer whereby the insurer promises to pay a sum of money upon the death of the insured to his or her designated beneficiary, in return for the periodic payment of money, known as a premium.

Life-Sustaining Treatment—Any medical treatment, procedure, or intervention that, in the judgment of the attending physician, when applied to the patient, would serve only to prolong the dying process where the patient has a terminal illness or injury, or would serve only to maintain the patient in a condition of permanent unconsciousness.

Limited Conservator—One appointed by the court to assist in managing the financial resources of a partially disabled person and one whose powers and duties have been specifically listed by court order.

Limited Guardian—A guardian with fewer than all the powers and duties of a full guardian and whose powers and duties have been specifically listed by court order.

Living Will—A declaration that states an individual's wishes concerning the use of extraordinary life support systems.

Long Term Care—The services provided at home or in an institutionalized setting to older persons who require medical or personal care for an extended period of time.

Long-Term Care Ombudsman—An independent advocate for nursing home residents.

Malfeasance—The commission of a wrongful act.

Malnutrition—A serious health problem caused by poor nutrition.

Mechanical ventilation—Mechanical ventilation is used to support or replace the function of the lungs by use of a machine called a ventilator that forces air into the lungs.

Medicaid—A federal program, financed by federal, state and local governments, intended to provide access to health care services for the poor.

Medical Malpractice—The failure of a physician to exercise that degree of skill and learning commonly applied under all the circumstances in the community by the average prudent reputable professional in the same field.

Medicare—The program governed by the Social Security Administration to provide medical and hospital coverage to the aged or disabled.

Mental Abuse—The intentional infliction of anguish, degradation, fear, or distress through verbal or nonverbal acts.

Minor—A person who has not yet reached the age of legal competence, which is designated as 18 in most states.

Misfeasance—Improper performance of a lawful act.

Motion—An application to the court requesting an order or ruling in favor of the applicant.

Narcotics—Generic term for any drug that dulls the senses or induces sleep and which commonly becomes addictive after prolonged use.

Neglect—Referring to a nursing home resident, the failure to provide a resident with the proper care needed to avoid harm or illness.

Negligence—The failure to exercise the degree of care that a reasonable person would exercise given the same circumstances.

Negligence Per Se—Conduct, whether of action or omission, which may be declared and treated as negligence without any argument or proof as to the particular surrounding circumstances, because it is contrary to the law.

Nominal Damages—A trivial sum of money which is awarded as recognition that a legal injury was sustained, although slight.

Non Obstante Verdicto (N.O.V.)—Latin for "notwithstanding the verdict." It refers to a judgment of the court that reverses the jury's verdict, based on the judge's determination that the verdict has no basis in law or is unsupported by the facts.

Notice of Petition—Written notice of a petitioner that a hearing will be held in a court to determine the relief requested in an annexed petition.

Nursing Home—A residential facility that gives nursing care or custodial care to an ill or injured person.

Nursing Home Abuse—The infliction of physical pain or injury on a nursing home resident by a person having care or custody over the resident.

Nursing Home Negligence—The failure to exercise the requisite standard of care in connection with the treatment and supervision of a nursing home resident.

Nursing Home Reform Act of 1987—Federal law governing nursing homes which gives nursing home residents certain rights.

Oath—A sworn declaration of the truth under penalty of perjury.

Objection—The process by which it is asserted that a particular question, or piece of evidence, is improper, and it is requested that the court rule upon the objectionable matter.

Ombudsman—Under certain state laws, an individual licensed to oversee various health care issues.

Out-of-Pocket Maximum—Refers to the maximum amount an insured may have to pay in coinsurance payments for covered services under the plan each year before the plan begins paying the full amount of covered services.

Pain and Suffering—Refers to damages recoverable against a wrongdoer which include physical or mental suffering.

Palliative care—A comprehensive approach to treating serious illness that focuses on the physical, psychological, spiritual, and existential needs of the patient—sometimes called "comfort care" or "hospice type care."

Parens Patriae—Latin for "parent of his country." Refers to the role of the state as guardian of legally disabled individuals.

Party—Person having a direct interest in a legal matter, transaction or proceeding.

Peer Review Organization (PRO)—The agencies responsible for ongoing review of the inpatient hospital care provided to people who are eligible for Medicare.

Permanent Unconsciousness—A condition that, to a reasonable degree of medical certainty: (1) will last permanently, without improvement; and (2) in which cognitive thought, sensation, purposeful action, social interaction, and awareness of self and environment are absent; and (3) which condition has existed for a period of time sufficient, in accordance with applicable professional standards, to make such a diagnosis; and (4) which condition is confirmed by a physician who is qualified and experienced in making such a diagnosis.

Person—An individual, corporation, business trust, estate, trust, partnership, association, joint venture, government, governmental subdivision or agency, or any other legal or commercial entity.

Personal Surety Bond—Bond executed by a guardian, and sureties willing to vouch for the guardian, that allows the court to seek restitution from the guardian or sureties if the guardian does not perform his or her duties.

Petition—A formal written request to a court, which initiates a special proceeding.

Petitioner—In a special proceeding, one who commences a formal written application, requesting some action or relief, addressed to a court for determination.

Petitioner—The person who files a petition with the court for guardianship or conservatorship.

Physician—A person licensed by the state to practice medicine.

Plan of Care—Refers to the comprehensive individualized care plan for residents required under the Nursing Home Reform Act of 1987.

Plaintiff—In a civil proceeding, the one who initially brings the lawsuit.

Pleadings—Refers to plaintiff's complaint which sets forth the facts of the cause of action, and defendant's answer that sets forth the responses and defenses to the allegations contained in the complaint.

Power of Attorney—A legal document authorizing another to act on one's behalf.

Post Mortem—Latin for "after death." Refers to the coroner's examination of a body to determine cause of death.

Prima Facie Case—A case which is sufficient on its face, being supported by at least the requisite minimum of evidence, and being free from palpable defects.

Primary Physician—A physician designated by an individual or the individual's agent, guardian, or surrogate, to have primary responsibility for the individual's health care or, in the absence of a designation or if the designated physician is not reasonably available, a physician who undertakes the responsibility.

Probate—Matter relating to or involving guardianship, the probate of a will, the estate of a decedent, or a trust.

Probate Court—Court with statutory authority to hear probate matters.

Procurement—The process of retrieving organs and/or tissue from a donor.

Professional Guardian—A public or private agency or organization that provides guardianship and/or conservatorship services and receives compensation.

Protected Person—A minor or individual for whom a conservator has been appointed or other protective orders.

Proximate Cause—That which, in a natural and continuous sequence, unbroken by any efficient intervening cause, produces injury, and without which the result would not have occurred.

Public Guardian—An individual employed by the state to act as a guardian and/or conservator when no private person or agency is available or able to act in this capacity.

Punitive Damages—Compensation in excess of compensatory damages that serves as a form of punishment to the wrongdoer who has exhibited malicious and willful misconduct.

Quality Improvement Organizations—Groups of practicing doctors and other health care experts that are paid by the Federal government to check and improve the care given to Medicare patients.

Question of Fact—The fact in dispute that is the province of the trier of fact, i.e. the judge or jury, to decide.

Question of Law—The question of law that is the province of the judge to decide.

Release—A document signed by one party, releasing claims he or she may have against another party, usually as part of a settlement agreement.

Relief—The remedies afforded a complainant by the court.

Representative Payee—Person who receives federal funds on behalf of another if the recipient is unable to manage their own finances.

Res Ipsa Loquitur—Literally, "the thing speaks for itself." Refers to an evidentiary rule which provides that negligence may be inferred from the fact that an accident occurred when such an occurrence would not ordinarily have happened in the absence of negligence, the cause of the occurrence was within the exclusive control of the defendant, and the plaintiff was in no way at fault.

Respiratory Arrest—The cessation of breathing, i.e., an event in which an individual stops breathing and if breathing is not restored, an individual's heart eventually will stop beating, resulting in cardiac arrest.

Respondent—The responding party, also known as the defendant.

Restatement of the Law—A series of volumes authored by the American Law Institute that tell what the law in a general area is, how it is changing, and what direction the authors think this change should take.

Restraints—Any method or device designed to restrict the movement of one's body.

Retainer Agreement—A contract between an attorney and the client stating the nature of the services to be rendered and the cost of the litigation.

Service of Process—The delivery of legal court documents, such as a complaint, to the defendant.

Settlement—An agreement by the parties to a dispute on a resolution of the claims, usually requiring some mutual action, such as payment of money in consideration of a release of claims.

Sexual Abuse—Nonconsensual sexual contact.

Skilled Nursing Care—A level of care that must be provided or supervised by a registered nurse.

Skilled Nursing Facility—A nursing facility with a staff and equipment able to give skilled nursing care.

Social Security Administration—The federal agency that issues retirement and disability benefits to qualified individuals.

Spending Down—The process by which an applicant for Medicaid benefits becomes or remains eligible by using up financial resources that are in excess of the limits set up by the Medicaid program.

Standby Guardian—A person nominated in a verified petition for voluntary appointment of a guardian to serve as guardian or upon future appointment by the court.

Statute—A law.

Substituted Judgment—The standard that guides the decision making of the guardian and entails making the decision the guardian believes the ward would make based on the ward's previously expressed preferences.

Successor Guardian or Conservator—A person appointed by the court to succeed a guardian or conservator upon death, resignation, removal, or incapacity. A successor guardian or conservator may also act in the case of an emergency if the acting guardian or conservator is unavailable.

Suicide—The deliberate termination of one's existence.

Summons—A mandate requiring the appearance of the defendant in an action under penalty of having judgment entered against him for failure to do so.

Surrogate—A person designated to make health care decisions for another individual if that individual is unable to make or communicate these decisions.

Survival Statute—A statute that preserves for a decedent's estate a cause of action for infliction of pain and suffering and related damages suffered up to the moment of death.

Terminal Illness—An incurable condition caused by injury, disease or illness which, regardless of the application of life-sustaining procedures would, within reasonable medical judgment, produce death and where the application of life-sustaining procedures serve only to postpone the moment of death of the patient.

Terminally Ill Patient—A patient whose death is imminent or whose condition, to a reasonable degree of medical certainty, is hopeless unless he or she is artificially supported through the use of life-sustaining procedures and which condition is confirmed by a physician who is qualified and experienced in making such a diagnosis.

Testamentary Appointment—An appointment of a guardian, conservator or power of attorney made by a will.

Testamentary Guardian or Conservator—A person named in the will of one who has been appointed by the court as guardian or conservator to succeed the guardian or conservator upon death.

Testator—A person who dies leaving a will.

Testify—The offering of a statement in a judicial proceeding, under oath and subject to the penalty of perjury.

Testimony—The sworn statement make by a witness in a judicial proceeding.

Tort—A private or civil wrong or injury, other than breach of contract, for which the court will provide a remedy in the form of an action for damages.

Tortfeasor—A wrong-doer.

Tortious Conduct—Wrongful conduct, whether of act or omission, of such a character as to subject the actor to liability under the law of torts.

Transcript—An official and certified copy of what transpired in court or at an out-of-court deposition.

Transplantation—The transfer of cells, tissues, or organs from an area of the body to another or from one organism to another.

Transplant Centers—Hospitals or medical centers that perform organ and/or tissue transplants.

Trial—The judicial procedure whereby disputes are determined based on the presentation of issues of law and fact. Issues of fact are decided by the trier of fact, either the judge or jury, and issues of law are decided by the judge.

Trial Court—The court of original jurisdiction over a particular matter.

Trust—A legal method used to manage and distribute property without a guardianship.

Unconstitutional—Refers to a statute which conflicts with the United States Constitution rendering it void.

Undue Influence—Abuse of position of trust in order to induce a person to do or refrain from doing something.

Unfit—Incompetent.

Uniform Laws—Laws that have been approved by the Commissioners on Uniform State Laws, and which are proposed to all state legislatures for consideration and adoption.

Venue—The proper place for trial of a lawsuit.

Verdict—The definitive answer given by the jury to the court concerning the matters of fact committed to the jury for their deliberation and determination.

Verification—The confirmation of the authenticity of a document, such as an affidavit.

Vicarious Liability—In tort law, refers to the liability assessed against one party due to the actions of another party.

Voluntary Arbitration—Arbitration that occurs by mutual and free consent of the parties.

Waiver—An intentional and voluntary surrender of a right.

Ward—A person over whom a guardian is appointed to manage his or her affairs.

Will—A legal document which a person executes setting forth their wishes as to the distribution of their property upon death.

Withholding or Withdrawing Treatment—Forgoing life-sustaining measures or discontinuing them after they have been used for a certain period of time.

Witness—One who testifies to what he has seen, heard, or otherwise observed.

Wrongful Death Action—An action brought to recover damages for the death of a person caused by the wrongful act or neglect of another.

Wrongful Death Statute—A statute that creates a cause of action for any wrongful act, neglect, or default that causes death.

Wrongful Life—In tort law, refers to the birth of a child that should not have occurred for some reason, e.g., the negligent performance of a sterilization procedure.

X—Refers to the mark that may be used to denote one's signature when the signer is unable to write his or her name.

BIBLIOGRAPHY AND ADDITIONAL RESOURCES

Black's Law Dictionary, Fifth Edition. St. Paul, MN: West Publishing Company, 1979.

Chen, Henry, The Mediation Approach: Representing Clients with Mental Illness in Civil Commitment Proceedings, *Georgetown Journal of Legal Ethics*, Washington, DC: Georgetown University Law Center, 2006.

Health Care Choices (Date Visited: December 2007) <http://www. healthcarechoices.org/>.

The Joint Commission (Date Visited: December 2007) <http://www. jcaho.org/>.

Judicial Council of California (Date Visited: December 2007) <http:// www.courtinfo.ca.gov/>.

National Academy of Elder Law Attorneys (Date Visited: December 2007) <http://www.naela.org/>.

National Conference of Commissioners on Uniform State Laws Law (Date Visited: December 2007) <http://www.nccusl.org/>.

National Health Law Program (Date Visited: December 2007) <http:// www.healthlaw.org/>.

National Institute on Aging (Date Visited: December 2007) <http://www. nia.nih.gov/>.

National Senior Citizens Law Center (Date Visited: December 2007) <http://www.nsclc.org/>.

New York State Unified Court System (Date Visited: December 2007) <http://www.nycourt.gov/>.

U.S. Department of Health and Human Services (Date Visited: December 2007) <http://www.hhs.gov/>.

U.S. Social Security Administration (Date Visited: December 2007) <http://www.ssa.gov/>.